Holy

Family

Christian Families in a Changing World

Robert J. Hater

TABOR
PUBLISHING

Valencia, California   Allen, Texas

Cover and Design: Cheryl Carrington

Unless otherwise noted, Scripture passages are taken from *The New American Bible with Revised New Testament* © 1970, 1986 by the Confraternity of Christian Doctrine, Washington, D.C. All rights reserved.

Send all inquiries to:
Tabor Publishing
25115 Avenue Stanford, Suite 130
Valencia, California 91355

Printed in the United States of America

ISBN 0-89505-685-2

1 2 3 4 5   92 91 90 89 88

*This book is dedicated to my parents Olivia and
Stanley Hater—the first heralds of faith in my life—and
to Tom, Mary Ann, and Joan, my brother and sisters.*

Contents

Introduction

Family life is changing. As this happens, new challenges, opportunities, and problems call Christians to examine the family from the perspective of their faith. In doing so, Christians will find happy and sad times in every family because life is an incomplete journey. The goal of this journey, which centers around love, is happiness. But the road to happiness often involves pain.

Popular piety often portrays the Holy Family of Jesus, Mary, and Joseph as the ideal family. In a parish discussion of family life, a participant commented, "I cannot identify with the Holy Family. My family can never be that perfect." This caused me to reexamine what, in fact, the Christian Scriptures actually say about Jesus' family. To my surprise, I found pictured a healthy yet broken family struggling to survive in troubled times. This is the image I offer as a model for today's families.

I began this book when I received a yearlong fellowship from the Center for the Study of Family Development directed by Dr. Patricia Voydanoff of the University of Dayton. This provided me with the time I needed to further reflect on the spirituality of the family and to put my thoughts in some kind of logical order. *Holy Family* is the result of these

efforts. It was written to help family members, catechists, and ministers view contemporary families in light of a new look at the Holy Family.

Before beginning this book, you should understand how the word *family* is used and what I mean by a healthy family. Family refers to "two or more people, united by common bonds, who share commitment, values, and traditions, and whose relationship is marked by some degree of permanence." Permanence can be experienced on a physical, psychological, or spiritual level.

In today's changing world, there are many kinds of family. The term *family* is normally used when referring to primary families, single-parent families, extended families, and blended or remarried families. The primary, or nuclear, family consists of either a husband and wife or a husband and wife with one or more children. In the single-parent family, children live with only one parent. The extended family includes the family's blood or adoptive relations. The blended or remarried family consists of members of two or more families, linked through subsequent bonding.

In a broader sense, family includes the freely bonded family, the Church family, Christian family, other religious families, the human family, and the family of God. The freely bonded family consists of chosen friends, not united by marriage, blood, or adoption, who fulfill the criteria for relational unity listed in the description of family. A religious community is an example of a freely bonded family. The Church family includes members of a religious denomination, congregation, or parish (Catholic, Methodist, Presbyterian, etc.). The Christian family embraces those who follow Jesus Christ. Other religious families include members of various world religions (for example, Jews, Buddhists, Hindus, etc.). The human family embraces all members of the human race. The family of God includes all creatures—humans, angels, and possibly creatures unknown to humankind—who share God's life and holiness. In the broadest sense possible, the family of God embraces all creation.

A healthy family is one that deals satisfactorily with brokenness and conflict. In this book, the words *broken* and *brokenness* are used metaphorically to mean "a condition of hurt, incompleteness, or tension." When applied to the family, brokenness can be viewed from a relational or personal viewpoint. Relational brokenness occurs when the structural relationships between family members break down. The condition of brokenness may be either temporary or permanent. It may result from sickness, temporary absence from the family, a failure to communicate, separation, divorce, or death.

Personal brokenness affects the entire family system and includes physical brokenness (sickness, starvation, or aging), moral or spiritual

brokenness (sin, guilt, or a sense of meaninglessness), and psychological brokenness (mental disorders, emotional stress, a sense of failure, or disappointments in life). Like relational brokenness, personal brokenness can be either temporary or permanent.

Now you are ready to begin your journey into this book, but it might be helpful for you to have a little descriptive map of what you are going to find. Remember that this book can be used for individual reflection or as the basis for group discussion and activity.

The first discovery you will make is that the Holy Family is a good model for today's changing families. Next, you will explore how the life experiences of Jesus extend the view of family beyond the primary family to a much broader interpretation of the family relationship. From this realization, you will see the family as a sacrament or as a visible sign of God's love.

You will then see how the family is the context for learning about God and for experiencing Church for the first time. Building on this context, you will see the family not as a deteriorating reality but as a great sign of hope for the future. And finally, you will see how parish life and ministry nourish families and are nourished by them.

This book is not a technical study of the family. It is intended for anyone who wants to reflect on the family from a Christian perspective. I have woven theological and pastoral insights with personal stories, none of which describe exact situations, except for stories from my own family. Each chapter includes questions for personal reflection or group discussion and family activities. The two-column format used in the book will help guide you through the book and provide suggestions for group use. I hope you enjoy exploring this book as much as I enjoyed writing it.

ONE

The Family of Jesus

Individual use. Find a comfortable place to read, where you can relax and not be disturbed. At the end of each section, there is a series of reflection questions. Have a pen or pencil ready to jot down your thoughts and reflections.

Group use. Have one or two Bibles, some pencils, and paper available for group use. When everyone has arrived and is comfortably seated, begin with a short prayer. Then introduce yourself, giving your name and the reason you joined this group. When everyone has been introduced, someone from the group reads the first section of this chapter.

I lived in Holy Family parish when the community celebrated its one-hundredth anniversary. At that time, I had the opportunity to page through old church records which portrayed a parish made up mostly of tightly knit German and Irish families living together in relative harmony. I noticed this picture began to change around 1975. No longer were "traditional" families with two parents and their children the only kind of family recognizable in the parish. As the divorce rate in the country rose, the parish became more sensitive to the needs of divorced people. Holy Family parish reached out to divorced people, helping them to feel welcome in the Catholic community. The parish also experienced a growth in pregnancies among unwed mothers. Holy Family parish wanted to help these women choose life for their unborn babies. Instead of sending them away, the parish opened its arms to them. As a result, single-parent families became more visible and active in the parish community.

Two-parent families were not immune from change. When the cost of living rose, many families found they needed two incomes to support themselves. Fewer families enjoyed the luxury of a full-time homemaker. Even when the family could survive on one income, many women realized they wanted to use their skills and talents outside of the home. At one time, these families could have counted on the extended family of grandparents or other relatives to help with child care and other responsibilities. Now families were more spread apart geographically, or relatives were not as available as before. These societal changes created tensions that prompted family members to learn new ways of coping.

Today, Holy Family parish has no average or typical family profile. As a result of evangelization efforts and community outreach, many Appalachian and black families, so integral to the region, are now a part of the parish family. The strong ethnic ties that once identified German and Irish families with the parish have loosened. Holy Family is now a multicultural parish family.

The transition from a rather homogeneous to a heterogeneous parish profile was not without tension. Change is always both exciting and threatening. Some families found it difficult to accept divorced people into the mainstream of the parish. They were afraid that such acceptance would send a message to young people that marital commitment is optional. Others, who experienced the pain of separation and divorce in their families, knew divorced families needed support from the faith community to recover and go on with life. Some people hesitated to invite Appalachian and black families into the parish because their life-style seemed different. Others enthusiastically welcomed the changes that occurred when new people became actively involved in liturgy and parish life. While some members left to find a parish that more closely resembled what they were accustomed to, most people stayed, weathered the changes, and became enriched by them. Today, Holy Family parish welcomes people, no matter what their ethnic background or family structure. It is not unlike many other parishes that adapted to change and expanded their boundaries to include a wide variety of people as family.

Individual use. These questions will help you think about how change has affected your family and parish over the past few years. Take some time to jot down your response to each question. If you like, share your responses with a relative, a spouse, or a friend.

Group use. Use any or all of the questions for group discussion.

1. What is the structure and ethnic background of your family?

2. How have societal changes affected your family?

3. What kinds of family exist in your parish community or neighborhood?

4. How has the makeup of the families in your parish or neighborhood changed over the years?

5. How has your parish or neighborhood adapted to these changes? What further adaptations still need to be made?

The Holy Family

Group use. Instead of reading this section aloud, divide the group in half. Have one group read Matthew 1:1—2:23 while the other group reads Luke 1:1—2:52. Be prepared to answer question 2 at the end of this section. Feel free to read through this section as you work. After a reasonable amount of time, come together and share your insights with one another.

The changes at Holy Family parish motivated me to reflect on the Holy Family and contemporary families in general. I asked myself, "Does the traditional image of the Holy Family symbolize today's families? Is there a way to look at the Holy Family that is faithful to Christian tradition and speaks to modern families?"

My reflections led me to the Christian Scriptures where I discovered new insights into the Holy Family that I feel speak powerfully to the needs of contemporary families. I learned that modern families can use the stories about the Holy Family for guidance in understanding, growth, and healing.

The traditional image of the Holy Family pictures Jesus, Mary, and Joseph as happy and loving people. Matthew's Gospel describes Joseph, Mary's husband, as a just man *(see* Matthew 1:20) who listens to God and makes difficult decisions based on his relationship with God. Mary's faith is strong enough to say yes to whatever God has in store for her *(see* Luke 1:26–38). She considers herself blessed by God and calls herself the Lord's handmaid *(see* Luke 1:48). Jesus is an obedient child with a strong self-image *(see* Luke 2:41–52). This image of the Holy

Family nourished many generations of closely knit families and still continues to guide family relationships.

As I carefully read the scriptural accounts of the Holy Family, I was surprised to find so much evidence of pain and brokenness in this family, especially during Jesus' conception, birth, and early adolescence. I realized that the combination of happiness and brokenness is consistent with Jesus' message of love. God cares for each person individually and wants all people to be happy. But the road to happiness often involves pain and suffering. God does not inflict pain, but rather helps people cope with life's tragedies. The Holy Family relied on this God of love to weather life's stormy moments.

By exploring the broken aspects of Jesus' family, today's families can better realize God's love for them and God's desire to heal family wounds. The infancy narratives provide a good starting point to ponder the joys and sufferings of the Holy Family.

Matthew and Luke are the only Gospel writers who provide records of Jesus' early life. Mark begins his Gospel with the public ministry of Jesus, and John starts his Gospel with a poetic description of how Jesus was the Word God spoke when creating the world. Only Matthew and Luke look at some events surrounding Jesus' birth and childhood.

As faith stories, the infancy narratives were not intended to provide exact historical information concerning Jesus' birth and childhood. Accuracy of detail, a concern of twentieth-century historians and news journalists, was not considered important by ancient writers. When Jesus lived, writers were more interested in capturing the meaning of the event than in reporting precise details. In fact, Matthew and Luke provide varying accounts of the birth of Jesus (*see* Matthew 1:1—2:23 and Luke 1:1—2:52). The infancy narratives are faith statements reflecting the early Christian belief in God's love for all humankind. The pain and hurt at the heart of the Holy Family is implied in both accounts, while God's love for the poor and needy is consistent with all four Gospel narratives. In the Holy Family, Christians have a model of a healthy family struggling through brokenness to discover freedom and peace.

Individual use. Use these questions to help you see what challenges the Holy Family faced and to reflect on how the Holy Family can be a model for your family.

1. Read Matthew 1:1—2:23 and Luke 1:1—2:52. What similarities and differences in the details of Jesus' birth do you note?

Group use. After the group members have finished discussing question 2, use question 3 for large group discussion. A break following this discussion would be fitting.

2. What problems did the Holy Family face during the conception and birth of Jesus? How did they handle these problems?

3. How are the problems faced by the Holy Family similar to problems experienced by contemporary families? by your family?

Family Roots

Group use. After a short break, each group member should use a piece of paper and a pencil to draw a family tree to the best of his or her ability and recollection. Then, have someone from the group read this section aloud.

People have always been fascinated with discovering their family roots. Knowing one's family history gives people a sense of belonging to something greater than themselves. Matthew and Luke offer accounts of Jesus' genealogy. Both evangelists trace Jesus' lineage through Joseph, a common practice in patriarchal cultures. Together they provide an interesting and revealing look at Jesus' ancestors.

Matthew traces Jesus' line back through David to Abraham. In doing so, he reminds the Christian community that Jesus' birth fulfills the messianic promises made to Abraham and to the royal house of David. Hence, there is a strong connection to Jesus' Jewish roots. Luke describes Jesus as the Son of God and shows that salvation in Jesus is extended to all humankind. Luke does this by tracing Jesus' roots all the way back to Adam, the father of humankind. In ancient times, genealogies illustrated a person's renowned ancestors. Matthew and Luke do this well in constructing Jesus' genealogy. Despite differences, both evangelists stress that Jesus was of Davidic descent, sprang from Joseph's line, and was conceived by the power of the Holy Spirit.

A curious element surfaces in Matthew's Gospel when one considers the questionable background of some of the people mentioned, for example, Judah and Tamar, Salmon and Rahab, Boaz and Ruth, David and Bathsheba (the wife of Uriah). From early Christian times, people wondered why certain people were included in the genealogy of Jesus. Consider the women mentioned above. Tamar deceived her father-in-law, Judah, into intercourse by masquerading as a temple prostitute *(see* Genesis 38). In folklore, Rahab was the prostitute of Jericho who gave shelter to the Israelites as they attempted to enter the Promised Land *(see* Joshua 2). Ruth was the Moabite woman who joined the Israelite community by being faithful to her mother-in-law after the death of her husband *(see* the Book of Ruth). Bathsheba was the wife of Uriah and a partner to King David's adultery *(see* 2 Samuel 11:6–27). Many of the men mentioned in the genealogy also had flawed backgrounds. Judah asked Tamar to have intercourse with him, thinking she was a temple prostitute. Sacred prostitution, a religious act honoring the goddess of fertility, was practiced in Canaan but condemned by the prophets. David was responsible for the death of Bathsheba's husband, Uriah. It is evident that some men and women in the genealogy of Jesus were sinners or foreigners. Their inclusion in Jesus' genealogy implies a broken condition in Jesus' ancestry and hints at the mystery of God's power to overcome any obstacle in preparing the world for the Savior. By including a wide variety of people with saintly and questionable backgrounds, Matthew sets the tone for the rest of his Gospel.

In general, the genealogies in Matthew and Luke indicate that Jesus assumed a broken human condition from the beginning of his life. By introducing their Gospels with Jesus' genealogy, Matthew and Luke establish a pattern which permeates all four Gospels—namely, that God is present in all human circumstances, works through different kinds of people, and heals broken lives.

Individual use. Use these questions to guide you in exploring the genealogy of Jesus and to help you ponder the meaning of your family roots.

1. Read Matthew 1:1–17 and Luke 3:23–38. Using the footnotes in your Bible or a dictionary of the Bible, research some of the people mentioned in Jesus' genealogy. What were they like as people?

Group use. After reading "Family Roots," use your family-tree sketch to discuss question 2 with the other group members.

2. Who are some of your ancestors on both your mother's and father's side of the family? What were they like as people? What kind of work did they do? What were their interests or hobbies? What does a knowledge of your family roots tell you about your family? about yourself?

3. Are some people alienated from your family? What are the reasons for the alienation?

Group use. If some members of the group are in stepfamily situations, discuss this question together.

4. What special challenges face a stepparent? How can Joseph's story help a stepparent deal with these challenges?

The Conception

Group use. Have someone in the group read this section aloud, or different people can take turns reading it while the other group members follow along.

The tension between happy, yet broken, family relationships surfaces when Joseph hears about Mary's pregnancy before their marriage *(see* Matthew 1:18–20). Matthew and Luke proclaim that this pregnancy is of the Holy Spirit and is not, therefore, the result of an ordinary conception *(see* Luke 1:26–38). The reader might ask, "Why was Jesus conceived during Mary's betrothal to Joseph and before the wedding feast?" The timing of Mary's pregnancy before marriage and the method of conception—through the Holy Spirit's power—might seem to some people a curious way of announcing Jesus' conception.

Jesus' conception has implications for today's families. God is present in various human situations—people living in poverty, abandoned spouses and children, unwed mothers and fathers, or people suffering the anguish of separation and divorce. Jesus was conceived under unusual circumstances. It is possible that gossip surrounded his family from the moment of his conception. If so, by trusting God, Mary and Joseph were able to survive the pain inflicted by some people who misjudged their situation. In these Gospel narratives, struggling families can find courage and hope in realizing that God's love can heal family wounds.

Luke pictures Mary as unmarried and pregnant, and describes her as confident that the child is of God. Regardless of her faith, Mary's struggle must have been tremendous. Alone and pregnant, she faces Joseph, her family, and friends with only the assurance that God is with her. She has no guarantees anyone will understand her predicament. Luke's Gospel implies that Mary's ambiguous situation follows her throughout her lifetime.

Luke emphasizes Mary's faith in her response to the angel *(see* Luke 1:26–38) and in her subsequent visit to Elizabeth *(see* Luke 1:39–56). The early Christian belief in the absolute need for faith is implied in the Visitation account. There Mary describes herself as the handmaid of the Lord. Through faith, God transforms Mary's fear, loneliness, and pain into hope, peace, and fruitfulness. The Magnificat *(see* Luke 1:46–55) complements the words Simeon spoke to Mary after Jesus' birth, "You yourself a sword will pierce so that the thoughts of many hearts may be revealed" *(Luke 2:35).* Luke depicts Mary as a struggling, faithful person. God's actions in her life symbolize the Christian call to be open to God, even in the midst of difficult situations. To respond as Mary did, a person must believe that God is always present, even when the future outcome is not clear.

Matthew concentrates on Joseph's dilemma after he discovers Mary is pregnant *(see* Matthew 1:18–25). While Joseph struggles to do the right thing, God enlightens him in a dream. Joseph trusts God and stands by his fiancée. Matthew describes Joseph as a faithful person who listens to God and trusts in an unknown future.

Mary and Joseph's struggle during Jesus' conception is the story of life. Their faith grew over the course of time as they listened to God. Their yes became stronger over the years because they believed in God's abiding presence.

Individual use. The Gospel stories of Jesus' conception can help you "hear" God's voice in your life. Use these questions to guide you in understanding the Scripture stories and to help you relate them to your life.

Group use. Break into two groups—one with men and the other with women. (If you are not in a coed group, one of the groups can represent the opposite sex.) Have the women use question 1 and the men, question 2 to see how Mary and Joseph may have responded to Jesus' conception. After both groups are finished, come together and discuss your responses.

1. Try to imagine Mary's feelings after the Annunciation. What is her greatest fear? her greatest hope? Then read Luke 1:39–55 to see how a member of Mary's family responded to her situation.

2. Try to imagine Joseph's feelings when he discovers that Mary is pregnant. What thoughts are running through his mind? What are his fears? hopes? Then read Matthew 1:18–25 to discover what convinced Joseph to stand by his fiancée.

3. Describe a time in your life when it was possible that members of your family did not understand something you had to do. How did you tell family members of your decision? How did they respond? How did you experience God's presence in this situation?

4. Have you ever had a dream that provided direction to your life or helped you understand a difficult situation better? If so, describe it.

5. There is an increase in teenage pregnancies throughout the United States. Do you know someone who is an unwed mother or father? How can the story of the Holy Family help an unwed parent have faith and hope?

The Birth of Jesus

Group use. Have someone in the group read this section aloud while the other group members follow along.

Jesus' birth marks a turning point in history because it shows a human family as the special focus of God's love. Jesus is born into an imperfect world, in impoverished circumstances. After Jesus' birth, the family flees to Egypt before returning home to Nazareth. While the family remains in exile, soldiers massacre innocent children. Much anguish and uncertainty about the future must have existed in Jesus' family. During these troubled times, however, Jesus' parents show an abiding trust in God's providence.

Whereas Matthew shows wise men bearing expensive and rare gifts to honor Jesus' birth, Luke has shepherds surrounding the young family. In Jesus' time, shepherds were poor and destitute. They often stole in order to survive and were not considered to be entirely trustworthy. By including shepherds at Jesus' birth, Luke depicts the poor and sinners as among the first to recognize the Savior of the world. Matthew, on the other hand, has wealthy astrologers traveling from distant places to pay the child homage. They look for a king and find one in the lowliest place. As Gentiles, the Magi are not part of the child's Jewish family. Matthew's story underlines the royal nature of Jesus' birth and emphasizes the role of nonfamily members in recognizing the importance of his birth.

The circumstances surrounding Jesus' birth into an imperfect world contain implications for contemporary families. God is present to all kinds of people—abandoned spouses and children, families who must leave their countries because of political or economic turmoil, the poor, the wealthy, non-Christians, and Christians alike.

Individual use. These questions will help you reflect on Jesus' birth and discover in the stories a way to find God in your family.

1. Read Luke 2:1–21 and Matthew 2:16–18. What were the circumstances surrounding the birth of Jesus? What values and strengths do you think emerged in the family as a result of Jesus' birth?

Group use. Choose question 2, 3, or 4 for group discussion.

2. What were the circumstances surrounding the birth of each member of your family? What values and strengths emerged as a result of each birth?

3. Do you know any persons or families who had to leave their homeland or neighborhood because of political or economic strife? If you do, what struggles did they face, and how did they deal with these struggles?

4. Which people, outside of your family circle, helped you recognize God's presence within your family? How did they do this?

Group use. This is a poignant story from the author's own life. Be sure to read it sometime after the meeting, in the privacy of your home. Review the family activities on page 23, and then end the meeting with the prayer on page 25.

Another Christmas Story

Whenever I recall the birth of Jesus, a sign of God's love for the human family, I remember another Christmas story. When I was a boy, my family owned a small dry-goods store in the West End of Cincinnati. It was a happy place where neighborhood folks laughed and cried together. Everyone bought merchandise there, knowing that all—including poor black and white people—were welcome.

One Christmas stands out above the rest. In early December, a delegation from the black Holiness church came into the store and asked for my father. I knew this was no ordinary meeting because Dad listened with a worried smile. When they left, he proudly told me they had invited him to preach the Christmas sermon at their church. "Dad," I asked, "what did you tell them?" He replied that he wanted to talk it over with Mom before giving them an answer.

I sensed what his decision would be—that the only sermon he could preach was in the store. The following Thursday, he confirmed my suspicions. Up the street he went to tell the church members he couldn't do it. He returned shortly, hoping they had understood him.

Two weeks passed, and it was the day before Christmas. Right before noon, Dad found out how well the people understood him. The church people came into the store carrying chicken dinners—a delicacy they occasionally brought us on busy days. Dad was overjoyed. As he thanked them, we all gathered around the potbellied stove. Dad threw in several large lumps of coal. The chill in the store was melted by the warmth of Christmas Eve, as everyone laughed, reminisced, and ate chicken.

Before the church people left, Dad moved about the store picking out a very nice selection of gifts, clothes, and household items for the church's poor who might not receive much on Christmas Day. As the coal turned to ashes, the real Christmas sermon was preached by the black and white brothers and sisters who exchanged best wishes for peace, joy, and goodwill.

The old store and church are gone now, but memories live on. Whenever I drive past the spot where they once stood, I remember the special Christmas that taught me the real reason for Jesus' birth.

The Christmas experience in my father's store, a symbol of God's love as demonstrated in Jesus' birth, helps me appreciate why Jesus was born in simplicity in the midst of poverty, uncertainty, and struggle. Jesus' birth, a paradigm of family life, shows how God's love can overcome human obstacles and bring new life. In recalling past Christmases, the only sermon I remember is the one preached in my family's store. This old store was my cave of Bethlehem. From it, I learned the real meaning of Jesus' birth.

Individual use. Everyone experiences Christmas differently. Take some time to remember your favorite Christmas story. These questions will help you reflect on the meaning of Christmas.

1.   How was Christmas Eve in the family dry-goods store a sermon?

2. Recall a Christmas story from your family history. How does it reflect the true meaning of Christmas as you understand it?

Activities

The following activities are offered as suggestions to enrich your family life. They relate to the main themes of this chapter and will help you put into action some of the ideas which may have occurred to you during the reflection and sharing time. Feel free to adapt the activities to meet the needs of your family, or create your own activities.

Neighborhood Picnic.   Gather together with several families and friends from your neighborhood or parish community for a picnic. Choose a location where people can run around and have fun. Ask the participants to bring food and music that represents their ethnic backgrounds. At some point during the picnic, gather everyone together to share a story that characterizes his or her family heritage.

Family Tree.   Use poster board or butcher paper to construct a family tree representing at least three generations of your family. If possible, place photos of each person on the family tree. Together, talk about what each member contributed to family life. Point out how members of the family resemble one another.

Healing Family Divisions.   Most families experience division and separation at some point. Think about a person in your family circle who may not be too involved with the family. Pray about this person, asking the Lord to show you the circumstances that may have contributed to this person's behavior. Ask the Lord to guide you in healing the relationship.

Unwed Mothers and Fathers.   If you have baby items not being used by the family, gather them together and donate them to the local Right-to-Life League or some other organization that helps pregnant mothers. If you have available time, consider volunteering to counsel unwed mothers and fathers.

Pregnancy.   If you are pregnant, begin to pray for the life growing inside of your womb. Teach other family members to touch your stomach and to pray for the emotional and physical health of the growing fetus.

Storytelling.   Begin to establish a custom where you share the story of each family member's birth on his or her birthday. Better yet, bring out the family picture album and go over the stories of birth in the family. Talk about who was present at each birth, how long the labor was, your feelings when each child was born. Do not forget to include grandparents and great-grandparents in the sharing. Talk about your hopes, desires, and even fears for the birthday person.

Moving.   If your family had to move (for social, political, or economic reasons), record the story of the move. Note the circumstances surrounding the move, the reasons the family made the decision to leave, the preparations for the journey, the "price" the family had to pay, and the final outcome. In recording the story, try to see how God was present throughout the move.

Celebrating Christmas.   Find out some of your family's Christmas customs by asking parents or grandparents to share them with you. Revive the ones you think your family will enjoy. Another idea is to begin a custom in which your family invites someone who is alone, or in some way neglected during this season, to share a Christmas meal with you.

The Feast of the Holy Family.   This often forgotten feast day falls on the **Sunday between Christmas and January 1.** Consider doing something special with your family on that day. Some ideas include going to brunch after Sunday Mass, bringing home a special pastry or fruit to celebrate the occasion, blessing your home, or visiting a relative, perhaps someone in a nursing home.

Prayer

The following prayer, the Magnificat, is taken from the Gospel according to Luke. It is based on several passages from the Hebrew Scriptures, including 1 Samuel 2:1–10. It has become a favorite prayer in the Church because of its deep emotion and strong conviction, and is used often in the Liturgy of the Hours.

Individual use. Incorporate this prayer into your family life. Write it out and hang it in an appropriate place, or use it as a mealtime or bedtime prayer with family members.

Group use. Close the session with this prayer. Have one person act as the leader, reading the passages marked *L*. Everyone else responds with the passages marked *R*.

L My soul proclaims the greatness of the Lord;
    my spirit rejoices in God my savior.
R For he has looked upon his handmaid's lowliness;
    behold, from now on will all ages call me blessed.
L The Mighty One has done great things for me,
    and holy is his name.
R His mercy is from age to age
    to those who fear him.
L He has shown might with his arm,
    dispersed the arrogant of mind and heart.
R He has thrown down the rulers from their thrones
    but lifted up the lowly.
L The hungry he has filled with good things;
    the rich he has sent away empty.
R He has helped Israel his servant,
    remembering his mercy,
L According to his promise to our fathers,
    to Abraham and to his descendants forever.

Luke 1:46–55

TWO

The Family of God

Individual use. This chapter will help you link your family to God's larger family. If you have a busy schedule, consider reading and reflecting on one section of the chapter at a time.

Group use. If possible, have newsprint or butcher paper, some pencils, and writing paper available for group use. Begin the session with each person sharing what his or her family did in the way of family activities since the last session. After about fifteen minutes of general sharing, have someone read this section.

A family begins when two people who share common bonds and values make a commitment to each other. Every family goes through a life cycle which involves transition points, challenges, and tasks to complete. Every family life cycle has its mountains and valleys, its moments of great joy, and its times of deep despair. The Book of Ecclesiastes may well have described the rhythm of the family when it claimed that there is an appointed time for everything under the heavens—a time to weep, and a time to laugh, a time to mourn, and a time to dance (*see* Ecclesiastes 3:1–8).

Mary and Joseph's family life began during the betrothal period when Jesus' conception was announced. The announcement certainly must have surprised many other family members. The couple, however, trusted God and communicated with each other. They began their family believing that God was truly with them. Although hardship surrounded Jesus' early life, the Holy Family stayed together and met very difficult challenges.

The infancy narratives say little about Jesus' early childhood other than the accounts of his birth, the days immediately following the birth, and the hasty, traumatic move to Egypt. The Gospel according to Luke, however, describes an incident that marks Jesus' transition from childhood to early adolescence. This event revolves around the family's visit to the Temple in Jerusalem when Jesus was twelve years old. The account contrasts Jesus' announcement that he must be about his Father's business with his parents' inability to understand why he failed to return with them after the Passover celebration. Mary asked Jesus, "Son, why have you done this to us? Your father and I have been looking for you with great anxiety" *(Luke 2:48)*. Jesus seems to rebuke his parents by responding, "Why were you looking for me? Did you not know that I must be in my Father's house?" *(Luke 2:49)*.

This story introduces a new element into the dynamic of Jesus' family. Up to this time, Joseph acted as Jesus' father. Now Jesus mentions another Father—one whom he must obey. Jesus' answer hints at the sword which the prophet Simeon predicted would pierce Mary's heart *(see* Luke 2:35). Jesus is beginning a process of separation from his family—a process that often marks a young person's entry into adolescence and young adulthood. The episode also suggests that Jesus' mother will have to face additional sorrows as her child matures and takes his own path in life. The story ends on a happy note, however, as Jesus returns home with his family and lives under the authority of Mary and Joseph.

The only story of Jesus' youth, then, contains a hint of conflict. The story recounts an episode in which Jesus upsets his parents and never really gives them a clear answer. Instead, he announces his special role in God's plan. When Jesus stands up to his parents in the Temple, he makes a powerful statement—that his calling from God takes precedence over family concerns.

The story of Jesus in the Temple informs the Christian community that the primary family is not a person's only goal. Another responsibility, one for which a family can prepare a person, is the call to follow God in fulfilling one's unique mission. In responding to God's call, a person may sometimes feel impelled to do something that will not be understood by other family members. Responding to this inner urge can be difficult, especially when close bonds tie family members together. Indeed, the decisions a person makes as a result of God's call may cause other family members turmoil and may even lead to a rupture in relationships. While the family prepares a person for God's special call, it must never stand in the way of that person's response. The story of Jesus in the Temple provides an example for Christians who struggle to make difficult decisions that may require taking an unpopular stance. Like Jesus, the Christian is expected to act with courage while respecting other people.

In another Gospel story involving a family scene, Mary asks her son to change water into wine at a wedding feast. Joseph appears to be out of the picture by this time. Tradition claims that Joseph died before Jesus began his public ministry. Jesus' response to his mother during the wedding feast at Cana complements his apparent reproach of her in the Temple. When Mary tells Jesus the banquet hosts are out of wine, he responds, "Woman, how does your concern affect me? My hour has not yet come" *(John 2:4)*.

It was most unusual for a Jewish man to call his mother "Woman." The term itself was commonly used during Jesus' lifetime, but it usually was reserved for acquaintances. By addressing his mother as "Woman," Jesus, once again, may be highlighting his greater mission in life. Nevertheless, Jesus responds to his mother's request. In doing so, he seems to rebuke her, because she does not appear to realize that his hour has not yet arrived. While Mary is concerned with helping a married couple avoid an embarrassing situation, Jesus sees his role in a broader perspective. Jesus responds to his mother's concern but, in the process, reminds her of more important tasks awaiting him.

Interestingly, in John's Gospel, Mary appears both at the beginning of Jesus' ministry, when he performs his first sign in Cana, and at the end of his ministry, when he is hanging on the cross. During his final hours, Jesus once again refers to Mary as "Woman," this time entrusting John, the beloved disciple, to her motherly care *(see* John 19:26–27). In John's Gospel, the moment of death is the hour to which Jesus referred while at the wedding feast. Here, at the cross, a new family is established. Both the Cana story and the account of Jesus' death as recorded in John's Gospel confirm what Luke depicted in the Temple. Although family members have no power over Jesus' response to his mission, they play an important role in his life. All three stories point to a family beyond the primary family—a family whose members can count Mary as their Mother.

Individual use. Now that you have finished reading about God's Family, take a few moments to write your answers to these questions.

1. Describe the early years of your family.

Group use. Take some time now to write your responses to these questions. Then, share your reflections with the other group members.

2. What common bonds and values do members of your family share with one another?

3. Recall one incident in your life when you did something that some or all family members disagreed with. In a few words, describe the circumstances. What were your reasons for taking this action? How did members of your family respond to your actions? What were the consequences?

Miguel

Group use. To introduce this section, have someone in the group read the first paragraph.

Group use. If someone in the group has a dramatic flair, have that person read this story. The other group members can close their eyes and picture the scene in their minds.

Jesus' actions in the Temple and during the wedding feast at Cana linked him to the family of God. By following in Jesus' footsteps, Christians continue to maintain allegiance to this family. Miguel's story shows how one Christian showed allegiance to God's family without sacrificing ties to his immediate and extended family.

I met Miguel at a conference for Mexican-Americans. This handsome man in his late twenties impressed me during our time together. The last time I spoke with him, we stood next to his car as we prepared to return home. He told me about his life in a small mining town. Pointing to his somewhat corroded automobile, he said, "Look at those marks all over the paint. I wonder what the mine fumes are doing to my insides if they do that to the paint on my car." I asked him why he stayed in the town. Miguel replied, "I could get a job somewhere else because I have a college education, but something more than money keeps me there. Our entire family lives near the mines and needs me. Besides, I work with the youth in town and coordinate the parish's social ministry. I also help the miners whenever I can. I feel God keeps me there."

Miguel is a key figure in his small mining town. Living for God's family, and capturing the spirit of Christ, he is prepared to sacrifice his health for what he sees as his vocation. Miguel is a person who lives for others. He symbolizes the challenge the Gospel presents to all believers.

Group use. After listening to the story, read the rest of this section to yourselves.

To claim that Jesus' message points to a call that extends beyond one's immediate family does not undermine the family's importance. Often the desire to reach out to other people begins within the family circle. Gospel values need to be incorporated into family life as much as they need to be lived out by God's family. Without family ministry, other parish activities would be ineffective and devoid of meaning. Ministering to the human family cannot be an excuse to neglect one's own family members.

Miguel saw a vital connection between his family obligations and the responsibilities to God's larger family. The support and love that Miguel received from his family provided a strong foundation and enabled him to reach out and help others.

Of course, there are family situations in which it is difficult to feel much support or nurturance. Perhaps an alcoholic or drug-dependent parent is unable to give the kind of love his or her children need. Or maybe the family situation is a violent one. People who come from such families can find love and acceptance in the larger family of God. After they have experienced love and support from the community, they can return to their families, bringing love and healing with them.

Everyone's situation is different, and no one's calling in life is the same. Each person, however, must learn to balance immediate family responsibilities with the demands of God's larger family. Failing to take into account either side of this equation is irresponsible. In Jesus and Miguel, Christians discover two responses to God's call. Each reflects a different time and place. Both persons honored family ties and, at the same time, extended their love beyond the immediate family to embrace God's larger family.

Jesus' claim on members of the Christian family is radical. He wants them to follow him *(see* Mark 1:16–20). When a disciple's father died, Jesus told his followers, "Follow me, and let the dead bury their dead" *(Matthew 8:22).* In fact, Gospel demands might severely tax family relationships. At one point during his ministry, Jesus harshly suggested that a son might be set against his father, a daughter against her mother, and a daughter-in-law against her mother-in-law *(see* Matthew 10:34). At times, family preferences must give way to other values, for Jesus said, "Whoever loves father or mother more than me is not worthy of me, and whoever loves son or daughter more than me is not worthy of me" *(Matthew 10:37).*

Gospel values relating to the broader family of God must be carefully discerned. Jesus never downplayed a person's responsibility to love one's own family. In fact, as a good Jew, Jesus faithfully observed the Law—central to which is loyalty to, and respect for, one's parents. Matthew shows Jesus reminding the Pharisees and scribes, "For God has said, 'Honor your father and your mother,' and, 'Whoever curses father or mother shall die' " *(Matthew 15:4).* Later in this passage, Jesus goes on to condemn those who minimize their responsibilities to parents by resorting to false interpretations of Jewish customs. Clearly, all members of God's family have a serious responsibility to their immediate family. At the same time, God's larger family sometimes may place great demands on a person's time and energy. Balancing these demands and responsibilities requires prudence, prayer, and a desire to listen to God.

Group use. When everyone has finished reading this section, use these questions as discussion starters.

Individual use. Record your answers to these questions, and then take some quiet time to pray about the many responsibilities you juggle in your life.

1. What responsibilities do you have to your immediate family? to your extended family?

2. What are your responsibilities as a member of God's family?

3. When and how do these responsibilities—to your immediate family and to the family of God—conflict?

4. How has prayer helped you resolve any conflict between responsibilities to your immediate family and to God's larger family?

Simplicity

Group use. Have one person from the group introduce this section by reading the first paragraph aloud to the other group members. After reading the first paragraph, discuss question 1 at the end of this section. After the discussion, read the rest of the section silently.

The infancy narratives depict Jesus' family as healthy, yet broken. The broken element is particularly significant because it portrays the Holy Family as a typically human family. This broken condition symbolizes the struggles every family endures. The fidelity of Jesus' family is a model for creating and nourishing strong family ties. The faith, trust, reverence, and obedience characterizing relationships within the Holy Family demonstrate the kind of family bonds needed to struggle with brokenness and doubt. The strong bonds within Jesus' small family helped him open his arms to the human family.

To relate one's own family to God's family, a person must become poor in spirit and develop a simple attitude. On one occasion, Jesus remarked, "Father, Lord of heaven and earth, to you I offer praise; for what you have hidden from the learned and the clever you have revealed to the merest children" *(Matthew 11:25)*. Jesus linked becoming like little children to following him when he said, "Amen, I say to you, unless you turn and become like children, you will not enter the kingdom of heaven" *(Matthew 18:3)*. In fact, Jesus concluded his discourse on the relationship between children and God's family with these words: "And whoever receives one child such as this in my name receives me" *(Matthew 18:5)*. It is hard to miss Jesus' message when he tells children to come to him, because "the kingdom of heaven belongs to such as these" *(Matthew 19:14)*.

The simplicity needed to appreciate God's love helps Christians see how their immediate families are connected to God's larger family. In God, all families on earth merge and find their common identity. Once, when Jesus was talking to a group of people, someone told Jesus that his mother and other family members wanted to speak with him. Jesus asked, "Who is my mother? Who are my brothers?" Pointing to his disciples, Jesus went on to say, "Here are my mother and my brothers. For whoever does the will of my heavenly Father is my brother, and sister, and mother" *(Matthew 12:47–50)*.

All human families are included in God's family. Everyone is a son or daughter, a sister or a brother. The person who follows God's call to serve this broader family will be blessed, for "everyone who has given up houses or brothers or sisters or father or mother or children or lands for the sake of my name will receive a hundred times more, and will inherit eternal life" *(Matthew 19:29)*. In God's larger family, primary family bonds fuse into the love that creates all human families.

A knowledge of God's family helps people see the relativity of all primary family relationships. The scriptural teaching on God's family encourages Christians to look at life from a new perspective. Human relationships and the use of material goods can be seen in a new light when family members recognize the entire human family as God's family. It takes a simple heart to understand the profound mystery of God's family.

Individual use. These are good questions to share with other family members.

1. How was the Holy Family a healthy, but broken, family? What are the implications for today's families?

Group use. Take a few minutes to write your responses to questions 2 and 3. Then choose a partner and share your answers. Conclude your discussion by saying a short prayer together.

2. How do you see your family as a healthy family?

3. What signs of brokenness or hurt can be detected in your family?

Group use. Use this question to brainstorm ways in which families can simplify their lives. If possible, record the group's ideas on butcher paper or newsprint. Afterward, take a break and enjoy one another's company.

4. How can you help members of your family develop a simple heart?

Group use. After the break, have one person from the group read the first paragraph aloud. Then ask someone else to read the story of Millie in a dramatic fashion.

Poverty of Spirit

The infancy narratives illustrate God's care for every person, especially the poor. Poor people often are a source of revelations of God's love. This can be seen in Millie's story.

One day, word came to the pastor of a downtown parish that a woman named Millie died. She had requested a Catholic burial, but no one at the rectory knew her. The funeral director said she was one of the many "bag ladies" in the large midwestern city.

As the priest prepared the funeral liturgy, he wondered if anyone would come. Shortly before the Mass began, he heard a great deal of noise in the church. Looking out from the sacristy, he saw beggars, alcoholics, bag ladies, and other street people assembling for the service. By homily time, they filled the church. Unable to account for what was happening, the priest discarded his prepared homily, walked to the center of the congregation, and asked, "Why are all of you here? Who was this woman?"

After a short silence, a beggar responded, "Millie was the kindest woman I ever knew. I loved her. She was always good to me." An alcoholic continued the story. "That's right! Millie gave me her coat when I was cold and sick." The bag ladies and the rest of the assembly nodded in agreement. They loved Millie as the "saint of the streets." That's why they came to her funeral. The street people knew Millie, even if the parish ministers did not. She gave what she owned to needy friends and loved them all deeply.

Later, the priest discovered Millie had seven children, none of whom attended the funeral. It seems that years before, a painful rupture in the family sent Millie into the streets. Her children never knew their mother had a spiritual conversion. They never met the street people, Millie's family during her last years.

Group use. You can read the rest of this section at home. For now, use questions 1 and 2 at the end of this section to spark a discussion on Millie's story.

Millie's story speaks of Jesus' announcement of good news to the poor. It recalls the episode in the synagogue at Nazareth when Jesus took the scrolls and read from the prophet Isaiah:

> "The Spirit of the Lord is upon me,
> because he has anointed me
>   to bring glad tidings to the poor.
> He has sent me to proclaim liberty to captives
>   and recovery of sight to the blind,
>   to let the oppressed go free,
> and to proclaim a year acceptable to the
>   Lord."
>
> *Luke 4:18–19*

Jesus spoke a message of hope to those without hope and revealed a God who is uniquely present to the poor and sinners. Millie's care for her street family gave witness to this God of love. God sent Jesus to bring good news to the poor, to proclaim liberty to captives, and to accomplish his mission through the forgiveness of sins. Jesus took on the oppression and rejection associated with poverty to show God's concern for needy people. Seeing Jesus born in poverty is the starting point for appreciating God's presence in the world.

The Christian Scriptures, however, never equate the poor with poverty. The poor are God's special friends. Poverty is an evil which must be overcome. To suffer physical, economic, psychological, or spiritual deprivation is poverty. Jesus' care centered on poor people, but he never canonized the poverty that burdened their lives. Perhaps every person exists in some condition of poverty. A person without food is poor (economic poverty). So is the individual who has cancer (physical poverty), or who is unable to control his or her anger (psychological poverty). Someone who has sinned or who finds little meaning in life is also poor (spiritual poverty). God wants to free all people from the poverty marking their existence.

Being poor does not, in itself, guarantee inner freedom. Poor people can be imprisoned by bitter and resentful feelings. To become free, a person must first become poor in spirit by trusting God, no matter what life brings. To be poor in spirit requires an attitude of simplicity in which a person opens his or her arms, like a trusting child, knowing God will be there.

1. Imagine yourself as the priest preparing to give a homily at Millie's funeral. After you have listened to the street people describing Millie, what would you tell them about God's love?

Individual use. These last two questions are good ones to discuss during a family meeting or as part of a meal-time conversation.

Group use. These last two questions are good ones to answer in the privacy of your own home. Be sure to include other family members in the discussion.

2. In what ways do you consider members of your family to be poor? What do you think are the roots of this poverty?

3. How can you become poor in spirit? How can this attitude help you and your family cope with today's changing world?

Forgiveness

Group use. Consider reading this section at home and using the forgiveness ritual on page 42 to conclude the meeting.

There is a popular saying, "To err is human, to forgive is divine." Anyone who has been deeply hurt by another person knows how difficult it is to forgive. It is often just as difficult to ask for forgiveness. Sometimes pride gets in the way, but, more often, the sinner loses self-respect and cannot accept forgiveness. Although people often condemn the offender, including the offender inside of themselves, God does not. Jesus revealed the depths of God's love by forgiving Peter, the friend who denied him in the hour of his greatest need *(see* Matthew 26:69–74). God's love for sinners continues today and is demonstrated in Eddie's story.

Late one afternoon, I popped into the rectory kitchen after a long meeting. I found a young man, calling himself Eddie, sitting at the kitchen table. He was very depressed and kept asking for a Bible, sackcloth, and ashes. I tried, without much success, to have him talk about what was bothering him. He just sat clutching the Bible I had given him, repeating that he must do penance. After an hour, he decided to leave. I knew he had no place to go, so I offered to find him a room for the night. He said no and left.

Within an hour, Eddie returned. I prepared some dinner for myself and offered Eddie some of it. "No, I'm fasting," he replied. And so it went for the rest of the evening. At eleven o'clock, he said he was leaving. "It's cold out there," I said. "Take care of yourself." He nodded and left. I went to bed.

At seven o'clock the next morning, I discovered Eddie back in the house. He was sleeping in the front room. When he heard me, Eddie sat up. He was in a deep state of depression and was unable to speak. I contacted a social worker who later called the police.

When Eddie saw the police officer, the tension ebbed from his body. He said to the officer, "Thank God, you came. I shot a man last week, and I think I killed him. I've been running ever since. Maybe now I will have some peace."

Eddie demonstrated symptoms of guilt and remorse. Unable to forgive himself, he could not admit his wrongdoing until a police officer arrived. Before that time, he had approached a Catholic priest, had asked for a Bible, and continued to fast. His request for sackcloth and ashes symbolized his spiritual poverty and gave evidence of his desire for repentance. Bound by sinfulness, Eddie was searching for inner freedom. Instinctively sensing God's love, he became a penitent and longed desperately for forgiveness. In retrospect, the external symbols of sorrow shown by Eddie were secondary to the change of heart that eventually would bring him peace and healing. God was with Eddie, leading him from sorrow to repentance.

In all three synoptic Gospels, Jesus accepted John's baptism of repentance *(see* Mark 1:9–11, Matthew 3:13–17, and Luke 3:21–22). Since Christians believe Jesus never sinned, it is safe to assume Jesus was baptized by John to underscore the importance of repentance. Sin is a source of spiritual poverty, and forgiveness is the key to overcoming this kind of poverty.

Throughout the Gospels, Jesus teaches that God forgives sins (for example, Luke 11:1–4 and Luke 15:4–7). But God expects sinners to return the favor by forgiving others. I learned this lesson in a powerful way one autumn day.

On the first cold day of the fall, I reached for my coat as I prepared to leave home to celebrate Mass. It wasn't in my closet. Anger filled me when I remembered where it was. "Darn it, he didn't return my coat," I thought. *He* was a man who had borrowed my coat, promising to return it in a few days. Now it was cold, and I was without my best coat.

When I entered church, the sacristan greeted me. My response was a muffled "Good morning," while I muttered to myself, "He didn't return my coat." Mass began, and I said, "Let us call to mind our sins." My insides boiled as I wondered why he hadn't returned my coat. I hardly heard the first reading and hadn't looked beforehand at the Gospel. My anger totally distracted me until I heard myself reading, "And Jesus said, 'To the man who takes your coat from you, do not refuse your tunic.' " I burst into laughter. The rest of the people in the church were probably wondering, "What's the matter with him?" When my laughter was finally under control, I told them the story of my coat and how the refusal to forgive had paralyzed me until I heard myself reading the Gospel passage.

I never did regain my coat. But after listening to the Gospel, I forgave the man who had borrowed it. At that moment, a miracle of healing began to work in me. The barriers came down, and I regained my composure. I learned an invaluable lesson. Because God forgives me, I can and must forgive others. Only in forgiveness does true peace come.

Forgiveness, the test of a person's response to God, reestablishes a harmony lost through sin or neglect. Throughout the Gospels, Jesus taught the need for reconciliation. Before healing the paralytic, he said, "Your sins are forgiven" *(see* Mark 2:1–12). And in the story of the prodigal son (also known as the story of the merciful father), Jesus showed the importance of forgiveness within the family. In fact, forgiveness is a great Christian family message. If Christians experience forgiveness at home, they will be better equipped to carry this important message of love into society.

Christians are pilgrims in the world. They will never have it "all together" until the end of time, when they meet God face-to-face in the power of the resurrection. In the meantime, inner peace depends on how Christians forgive and accept forgiveness. Only by forgiving and accepting forgiveness can people truly experience the freedom that all sons and daughters of a loving God are invited to accept. Only by forgiving others and accepting forgiveness can all people live in harmony.

1. Recall a time when a family member showed symptoms of guilt and remorse. Describe his or her actions. Were you able to recognize these symptoms for what they were? What did you do to help the person? How was harmony restored?

2. When did a passage from Scripture or a homily help you recognize your need to forgive someone who hurt you? Briefly tell how you were able to forgive the person after hearing God's Word.

3. Read Luke 15:11–32. In a few words, describe how each family member was hurt. How did each family member respond to the younger son's return? Which way of responding is closest to the way you would have responded?

4. After you read Luke 15:11–32, imagine the two brothers meeting face-to-face. What do they say to each other? Write the dialog here or on a separate sheet of paper.

Activities

Individual and group use. Choose at least one of these activities to use with your family, or create one of your own.

The following activities are designed to help you and your family enact the basic principles described in this chapter. Since this chapter focuses on God's family, consider inviting some friends or neighbors to participate in your family activity.

Family Life Cycle Chart.   Use butcher paper or poster board to construct a chart of your family life cycle. Think about the major seasons of the family, such as the courtship period, the early years, the birth of children, the teen years, the empty-nest years, broken times, and the like. Divide the chart according to the number of seasons you identify. Use words, pictures, and photographs to describe each period in your family's life. Don't forget to leave some space to add to the chart as the family continues its journey.

Separation Ritual. There are natural times when separation happens within a family's life cycle—when a child first begins school, after a graduation from high school or college, during a divorce, as an elderly parent approaches death, and so on. It is not always easy to let go. If your family is nearing a time of separation, create a family ritual to help ease the transition. For example, if a child is entering school for the first time, gather the family together and ask the older family members to share experiences of their first day at school. The stories should be true to life and positive. No one should be afraid to share painful experiences, but an effort should be made to show how something positive came from each struggle. After sharing, each person can give the child something symbolizing a new era in the child's life. For example, an older brother or sister can give the younger child his or her old pencil case. At the end of the ritual, share some ice cream together.

Meeting of the Clan. If a family member is struggling with an important decision, gather the family together for a clan meeting. Even small children should be included. If possible, include members of the extended family as well as close friends of the struggling individual. Open the meeting with a short prayer or a reading from Scripture, such as 1 Corinthians 2:10–16. Then have the struggling person briefly describe the situation. If the gathering is large, the group can break into smaller groups to brainstorm ways to help the family member. These possibilities can then be presented to the struggling individual. Finally, the person chooses the most helpful suggestions. The meeting ends with the family pledging its support in some concrete way.

Reaching Out. As a family, take a look at your neighborhood community and identify one problem that needs attention or one person who needs help or support. Develop a plan of action, and decide how each family member can contribute to it.

Exploring the Family Life-style. Hold a family meeting to discuss the budget. Make a list of the material things you hope to buy for the family within the next year. Each person should make a copy of the list and check off one or two items that he or she considers essential. Older family members can help children who cannot read. Then, discuss your choices, and decide which items on the list are essential and which items are nonessential, but nice to have. Decide what the family will do with the money saved by not buying nonessential items.

Forgiveness Ritual. The following ritual needs to be handled very delicately and should not be used without a preliminary discussion or without the willingness to follow up on any pains that might surface. If you decide the ritual may cause more pain than healing, do not use it. When used sensitively, this activity can be a moving family celebration.

        Have all family members come together. Give each person a sheet of paper and a pencil. Have everyone draw a circle in the middle of the paper and write his or her name in the center of the circle. Then ask everyone to draw a circle for each family member and write the person's name inside the circle. These circles should be drawn either near the center circle or away from it, depending on how close or distant the person feels to the various family members. Be sure to indicate how family members may feel close to someone on some days and more distant at other times. Reassure family members that feeling close or distant to someone does not indicate that a parent or child loves one person more than another. Then ask the family members to draw a box around the circle that is the farthest from the center circle and write down the reasons for the distance. Smaller children can draw a picture to describe the situation. Then ask each person to think about ways to bridge the distance. Whoever wishes to do so may share his or her thoughts with the others. Discuss ways to become closer as a family. End the activity with a prayer for forgiveness and some sort of family celebration—hugs, kisses, a small party, or perhaps a family outing.

Prayer

The following prayer is attributed to Saint Francis of Assisi who lived from 1181–1226. A favorite saint of many people, Saint Francis is an example of someone who renounced the materialistic values of his family in order to respond to the needs of God's larger family, especially its poorest members. This prayer beautifully speaks of the saint's desire to reach out to other people by being poor in spirit, loving, and forgiving.

Individual use. During the next week, use this prayer as an examination of conscience. Resolve to improve where growth is needed. Rejoice in the strengths you demonstrate.

Group use. Use this prayer at the end of the forgiveness ritual. If the group members know the song version, sing it together.

Lord, make me an instrument of your peace.
Where there is hatred, let me sow love;
    where there is injury, pardon;
    where there is doubt, faith;
    where there is despair, hope;
    where there is darkness, light;
    and where there is sadness, joy.

O Divine Master, grant that I may not seek so much
    to be consoled as to console,
    to be understood as to understand,
    to be loved as to love.

For it is in giving that we receive,
    it is in pardoning that we are pardoned,
    and it is in dying that we are born to eternal life.

THREE

The Family as Sacrament

Individual use. This chapter helps you see the family as a sign and symbol of God's presence in the world.

Group use. Begin by having each person share one thing that happened during the week to make him or her conscious of God's presence in the family. After everyone has shared, have someone read the first two paragraphs. Then turn to page 47 and discuss question 1. List the suggested definitions on newsprint or butcher paper. Return to the text and allow the group about five minutes to finish reading this section by themselves.

Saint Augustine once described a sacrament as "a visible sign of invisible grace." Put in more contemporary language, a sacrament is a way of experiencing God's presence in the world. To call the family a sacrament of God's love presupposes that life is a mystery—incomplete and imperfect—yet moving toward fulfillment. In an incomplete world, God helps imperfect people move toward happier times.

To call the family a sacrament may sound strange to people who associate sacrament with the seven sacraments of the Church—Baptism, Confirmation, Eucharist, Penance, Matrimony, Holy Orders, and the Anointing of the Sick. The Second Vatican Council helped broaden the Church's understanding of sacrament by returning to a more ancient appreciation of the term.

The early Christian communities did not use the term *sacrament* but spoke instead of celebrating the sacred mysteries. These mysteries centered around Jesus' life, death, resurrection, and continued presence in the community. The term *mystery* was not restricted to liturgical usage but also embraced the mystery of God's love made manifest in people's lives. Tertullian translated *mysterion* (the Greek word for mystery) as *sacramentum* (the Latin word for sacrament). Augustine and other Church leaders soon accepted Tertullian's term to refer to the many ways God's love is manifested in people and in the Church. It was not until the Middle Ages that the term *sacrament* became restricted almost exclusively to mean the seven sacraments.

Vatican II restored some of the original meaning to the word *sacrament* by linking the principle of sacramentality to God's unfolding love, especially as it is manifested in the person of Jesus Christ and in the Christian community. The *Constitution on the Sacred Liturgy* declares, "For it was from the side of Christ as he slept the sleep of death upon the cross that there came forth 'the wondrous sacrament of the whole Church' " *(#5)*.

Jesus Christ is the chief sacrament. For all Christians, the best and most complete way of encountering God in today's world is through the person of Jesus Christ, the fullest expression of God's love. The Church, the Body of Christ on earth, becomes the visible sign of Jesus' presence in the world. God's sacramental love in the family flows directly and indirectly from Jesus' life in the Christian community. The seven sacraments nourish this life and enable the Church, including the many families who make up the Church, to be a visible sign of God's loving presence in the world.

During my father's illness, two events symbolized how my family was a sacrament—a sign of God's love. The first event happened on the last Easter Sunday of Dad's life. The details have faded, but I will always remember the Easter when God gave me a powerful glimpse of love.

The Alleluia of Easter rang in our family. After four months in the hospital, Dad was home. It was as if our family had climbed to the top of a mountain and was looking at the valleys below, remembering the pain, sleepless nights, and broken dreams. The path up this Easter mountain had been narrow. Sometimes we stumbled and wanted to turn back, but we stuck together as a family and finally reached the top.

Simplicity marked our Easter song. Its tune began in the early afternoon when Dad, Mom, and the rest of our family celebrated Eucharist in our living room. Dad's weak voice spoke the prayer of our hearts, "Let us pray for God's blessings and goodness to us." Dad's peace, after much intense suffering, allowed the overpowering presence of God's love to fill us with joy.

Simplicity also describes how the small grandchildren approached Dad, as if he were a sanctuary. When he smiled and extended his faltering arms, they ran to gather around him, just like the children must have gathered around Jesus. The adults watched in silence. Easter's Alleluia blessed each of us, as Dad and the children became a sacrament of God's love to us.

The memory of Dad's last Easter joins with another one. I experienced this second event, which took place at Dad's grave, as the fulfillment of his earthly journey. This is how I remember that sacred occasion.

I stood at Dad's grave eight months after his death. A big oak tree nearby provided a strong backdrop for the large crucifix that stood a few yards behind his gravemarker. The sunlight sparkled through the oak leaves and changed the darkness of death to the brightness of new life. Suddenly, a powerful, warm feeling filled me, and I experienced a profound peace. Dad was with me. His body lay at my feet, but his spirit filled my heart. God and Dad were together. I heard my father speak, as his voice seemed to join with God's in saying these words of peace: "Bob, I am with God, who is stronger than anything. Let go of earthly concerns and be with me and God. Go in peace. I am with you."

Peace and joy overwhelmed me. I wanted to remain rooted to that spot forever. Finally, however, I said a short prayer and walked away. As the sun illuminated my path, I remembered the words, "Love is stronger than death. . . . It is a flash of fire, a flame of Yahweh" (*see* Song of Songs 8:6–7). At my father's grave, I experienced a reality toward which all life moves. I now appreciate better how the family is truly a sign of God's love and care.

Group use. After everyone has had ample time to read this section, return to the group's definitions of sacrament. Discuss how the ideas suggested by the group were affirmed or altered by reading this section.

Individual use. Take some time now to mull over what you have just read. Use the reflection questions to record your thoughts, memories, and feelings.

1. What is your definition of a sacrament?

2. Recall one story from your family history that shows how family is a sacrament. In a few words, describe the event and tell how you experienced God's presence through it.

Group use. Take some more quiet time now to read the next section of this chapter.

Finding God in Life

From the earliest times, people have discovered God through the beauty of a sunset, the force of an ocean, or a mountain's majesty. God's presence is felt in both the joyful and painful events of life. Since life reveals the Creator, people better appreciate God and themselves whenever they cherish life. Family sacramentality, rooted in life, discloses God's love. I discovered this essential truth in conversations with a young woman.

Shelly, a college student, often asked me questions about God. She never spoke about her religious background, but her goodness and sincerity impressed me. Once I asked her if she belonged to any church. To my surprise, Shelly confided that she had been to church only twice in her life and had never bothered to join any particular religious denomination. "But," she added, "from childhood, my parents taught me to discover joy in a flower or a setting sun, to respect life, and to be kind to all people, especially the poor."

Shelly eventually embraced the Christian faith. As we continued our conversations over the course of time, she realized that her parents had taught her about God without using God's name. Their attitude toward life helped God's sacramental presence to enter her heart. The basic goodness I first perceived in Shelly had its roots in her early childhood experiences. Her parents may never have taught her about God in a formal way, but Shelly's upbringing prepared her later to discover God in the Christian faith. Now Shelly thanks her parents for their love and goodness which rooted her newfound faith. From her childhood experiences, Shelley learned that an appreciation of God comes from life itself.

Birth begins a process which discloses God's love. This love is exposed while feeding a child, caring for a sick parent, sharing intimacy, celebrating a birthday, or watching children play. In happy times, family sacramentality speaks of the goodness built into the very fiber of human relationships. I discovered the sacramental value of family relationships when I attended a birthday party for an eighty-year-old woman.

Marie had ten brothers and sisters. Only three of them were still alive. Her children gave her a special present for her birthday—a four-day family reunion. Seventy relatives came. On Saturday evening, we celebrated Mass and then gathered for dinner. Afterward, family members—young and old alike—recalled happy times together. Love and respect poured forth in a way that disclosed how this family uniquely revealed God's presence.

The evening I spent with Marie's family is repeated a thousand times in most families. These special moments have a way of revealing the joys and hopes that exist along with life's struggles, moving family members to a deeper sense of unity and peace.

It is important to remember happy times, especially when life becomes almost unbearable. I remember getting a phone call early one morning. A friend asked me in a troubled voice, "Did you hear that Ray died last evening?" I replied, "No, what happened?" My friend did not

know. Ray, his wife Nancy, and their three children were my friends. Later in the day, I discovered that this healthy man in his early forties had been getting ready for bed when he gasped slightly and died. That was it. "So quick and yet so tragic," I thought.

I called the family and offered to help them face the future. No one can explain to Ray's family why he died early in his life, leaving a beautiful family devastated and his friends bereft. But his family and friends can keep their memories of him alive. By helping each other cope with feelings of loss and sorrow, Ray's friends and family share the bonds of love that tied them together in the first place.

God can be found in the daily events of life. The seven sacraments of the Church take common, ordinary experiences and raise them to a higher level of meaning. Shelly's parents taught their daughter to value life and to find joy in creation. This attitude toward life later helped her find God in the Christian faith and celebrate the joy of life in the sacrament of Baptism. Marie's family had a long history and several generations of people with whom to share it. In celebrating the sacrament of Eucharist, the family recalled Jesus Christ's passion, death, and resurrection. After Mass, the family found God anew in shared memories and family stories. Ray's family felt comfort in the Mass of the Resurrection and healing in the community's supportive response. These three stories demonstrate God's loving presence to people. In all three scenarios, the family was a sacrament—a visible sign of invisible grace. These family experiences, in turn, provided an environment in which members could experience the Church's sacraments in more profound ways.

Individual use. After you have read this section and answered the reflection questions, consider involving your family or friends in the "Creation Walk" activity described on page 61.

Group use. When everyone is finished reading, use any or all of these questions to begin a group discussion. After the discussion, take a short break and enjoy one another's company.

1. When and how have you experienced God in creation?

2. How did your parent(s) or other family members prepare you to discover God?

3. In which daily events of life do you experience God's presence?

4. How have life experiences enhanced your understanding and appreciation of the seven sacraments?

Matrimony

Group use. Now that the break is over, and everyone is back together again, have someone from the group read aloud the first two paragraphs of this section while everyone else listens or follows along in the text.

In his Apostolic Exhortation *On the Family,* Pope John Paul II describes marriage in terms of communion and covenant.

The first communion is the one which is established and which develops between husband and wife: By virtue of the covenant of married life, the man and woman "are no longer two but one flesh" and they are called to grow continually in their communion through day-to-day fidelity to their marriage promise of total mutual self-giving *(#19).*

Marriage, a covenant which begins when a husband and wife pledge their mutual trust, fidelity, and love, is one of the seven sacraments of the Church. In a real way, this sacrament can be called the sacrament of the family because, on their wedding day, husband and wife begin to live as a family. This family—with or without children—lasts forever. The death of a spouse does not destroy a family, even though it changes the family focus. Divorce, likewise, does not end a family, although it changes its structure. Parents and children separated by divorce are still a family with responsibilities to one another. Although acquaintanceships and friendships might end, family relationships continue forever. As a sign of God's love, the sacrament of the family links the primary family to God's larger family through permanent bonds. Neither death, nor divorce, nor neglect can destroy these bonds.

Group use. Before you continue with the text, choose a partner and use the "Reflections on a Dream" activity (page 62) to share your past and present hopes and dreams about having a family. Listen attentively to each other. This is a time for sharing—not a time to offer suggestions or advice. When you are finished sharing, spend some quiet time reading through the rest of the section.

When two people marry in Christ, they seek to fulfill their calling by pledging to proclaim God's love through love and sacrifice. Because each family possesses unique gifts, it will fulfill this vocation differently. The Edwards family, for example, is happy and carefree. Walking into their home is like going to a rummage sale. One never knows what to expect, for the family members are not too concerned about the condition of the house. But they live life with great exuberance, joy, and love. Neighbors who want to have a fun time are sure to find it in the Edwards household.

On the other hand, the Raymond family is organized and tidy. The family knows how to have fun but in a different way than the Edwards family. In fact, in comparison to the Edwards family, the Raymond family appears stiff. Although they are polite and formal, their hospitality will make any visitor feel special. Both families have something unique to offer in carrying out their special mission. In two very different ways, God's presence is made known to the world.

Since a family will never be repeated, each family reveals God's love in a unique way. A divorced family sacramentalizes this love differently from a primary family consisting of a mother, father, and children. A childless family offers something that a large-sized family cannot duplicate. Like an individual person, each family has its own special "fingerprint," whose overall design gives a clue to God's presence in the world.

As a sacrament of God's love, the family develops through a process of steady growth. People marry, children are born or added to the family, families mature, and members separate to begin their own families. Depending on how families develop over time, this process leads to the formation of either deep or superficial relationships. Family life does not automatically guarantee strong bonds as people grow older.

Families also change through traumatic events, such as the divorce or the death of one of its members. Such events cause family patterns to shift dramatically. Both gradual and radical changes in family structure affect how families experience God's love. Marcia told me how a traumatic change affected her family and her relationship with God.

"I came from a happy family," Marcia began, "and for years after my marriage to Bill, our life went well. During that time, I never thought seriously about whether God loved me or not. After our second child, Bill lost his job. He started to act differently. He became sullen and stayed away at night. He began drinking heavily and abusing me and the children. Finally, he left home, and we eventually divorced."

Marcia then reflected on her attitude toward God. "At first, when Bill started to change," she continued, "I became angry with God and wondered why God had abandoned us. Only gradually did I feel the Lord's special presence in the struggle. By the time the divorce proceedings began, I experienced God in a new way—as sustaining me. My trust in God and life enabled me to survive. Later, I obtained a Church annulment of my marriage to Bill and remarried into a blended family. Now God comes to our family through deeply shared care and affection."

Marcia said she experienced a giftedness in family life even during the rough times, and she now sees goodness in Bill despite his failings. The gifts Marcia recognized in the family she began with Bill and in her blended family filled her with hope and encouragement.

Like the Holy Family, all families must confront struggles and broken moments. Especially in painful circumstances, people need to identify their special family resources and gifts. In doing so, family members can experience God. Sometimes it is difficult to recognize family gifts when a youth on drugs fails to improve, an alcoholic spouse neglects to get proper treatment, or spouses fail to communicate with each other. In such circumstances, viewing Jesus as the servant-healer helps put God's presence in a new perspective. The image of Jesus as one who suffered helps family members caught in painful situations to identify with the broken Christ. Jesus is a powerful sign of a God who dwells with hurting people. He invites them to become servant-healers. Jim's story taught me the power of this image.

Jim's wife ran away with another man, abandoning her husband and three sons. Jim's faith carried him through the initial hurt and anger, and gradually helped him to forgive her. As a single parent, he developed deep bonds with his three sons, which helped to heal the wounds inflicted by the mother's departure. Today, Jim's boys rarely see their mom, but they are healthy, stable young men.

Recently, I talked with Jim about his struggle. He said, "When it first happened, I survived by picturing myself on the cross. During this time, I underwent a kind of death. As the months passed, I realized that love must overcome hurt, especially for the sake of my sons. This has happened. Today, they are ready for life, and I am at peace."

In seeking God in the midst of pain, Jim showed his sons the meaning of love and forgiveness. These four men enjoy unique gifts as a family. Because of Jim's example, his sons are ready to live a full life. Without their father's love, they might have become tragic people. Authentic witness to God's love never happens without tension, for family gifts always develop in life's ambiguous crucible. The family becomes a sign of God's love most effectively by living the values Jesus taught.

Group use. Use any or all of these questions as discussion starters.

1. How has your family developed over time? In the space below, draw a chart of your family's development from its beginnings to now. Include dates and important transition points.

Individual use. It would be interesting to ask other family members how they would answer this question and to compare their answers with your own.

2. How would you describe your family to a stranger? How do you think an outside observer would describe your family?

3. What family situations get in the way of your being able to experience God's presence?

4. Read Matthew 5:1–16. Then, in the space below, write one beatitude that describes how your family is both blessed and a blessing to others. Be creative! You are not limited by the choices offered in Matthew's Gospel.

5. When has a member of your family acted as a servant-healer? Briefly describe the circumstances and show how the family member was able to heal others as a result of personal suffering.

God's Saving Presence

Group use. This is an important but long section. To get the most benefits from it, read it at home and answer the reflection questions sometime during the week. Skip now to "Eucharist" on page 59.

Family sacramentality flows from the sacramentality rooted in life. To limit an understanding of the family to a functional analysis misses life's deepest dimensions which both begin and end in mystery. But within the unfolding mystery of salvation, key ways in which the family reveals God's presence can be discovered. This is particularly evident in the family's communal life, its growth in holiness, and its ability to give selflessly out of love for one another.

Every family possesses unique gifts that are influenced by the family's history, cultural background, work experiences, responsibilities, and faith life. Providing a universal list of family gifts is never possible. Because each family is different, it is necessary to focus instead on family uniqueness to appreciate how each family sacramentalizes God's love. This uniqueness implies that each family represents a unified whole, incorporating the gifts and talents of individual members. In other words, the family is more than a group of individuals. It is a dynamic system in which each person influences, and is influenced by, other family members. Thus, God's presence in individual family members can never be dissociated from God's presence in the total family unit.

God's love as revealed in creation, the person of Jesus, and human relationships inspires family members to love, to care for, to forgive, and to trust one another. In doing so, the family grows in holiness. Holiness, a term seldom used in contemporary language—even religious language—is central to both Jewish and Christian understandings of God.

The first creation account to appear in the Bible distinguishes between what is good and what is holy *(see* Genesis 1:1—2:4). All creation is good. After each day, "God saw that it was good," and on the sixth day, after creating man and woman, God saw that it was "very good" *(Genesis 2:3).* Finally, on the seventh day, which is called holy, God rested from the work of creation *(see* Genesis 2:3). The priestly account of creation, which is probably rooted in Jewish liturgy, implies two profound beliefs symbolized in the Sabbath rest: (1) holiness is God's own life, and (2) human beings created in God's image and likeness bring holiness into the world.

In the early stages of biblical thought, the word *holy (kadosh)* meant "set apart." This did not mean that the nation Israel, which is described as holy, was isolated from the rest of the world. Instead, it meant that Israel was special—it had a unique role to play in the history of salvation. In the Book of Hosea, holiness implies God's presence within a person *(see* Hosea 11:9). According to the Jewish scholar Rabbi Abraham Heschel, holiness characterizes earthly endeavors and is reflected more in simple deeds than in public ceremonies. Consequently, human beings are the source and the initiators of holiness in today's world. Holy families convey God's holiness in ways that give greater meaning to public celebrations.

The Christian tradition, rooted in the Jewish faith, teaches people that life is good and that God calls family members to holiness. The linking of life's goodness with holiness happens in the most ordinary ways. I remember an incident at Christmastime one year that brought home to me these simple truths.

One day in church, I noticed Edna and her five-year-old grandson Billy by the manger. As little Billy pointed to each of the figures, his grandmother told him the Christmas story. Watching them, I realized how most people learn about God from ordinary, holy people like Billy's grandmother. Holy people come in all sizes and shapes, but they have one feature in common. They are simple people who look like my mom and your dad. They sound like my sister and your brother. Without these simple, holy people, there would be no Church. It was simple, ordinary folk who first gave the world the Christmas story. From holy people, Christians learn religious traditions, faith, and life's holy purpose. Billy learned the Christmas story from Grandma Edna, who first learned holiness from other holy Christians like herself.

Holy people testify to God's holiness. Alone, humans cannot show God's holiness. Too much evil, injustice, and pain exist in the world for individuals alone to reveal God's goodness. That is why the Hebrew Scriptures suggest that people are saved together. This communal dimension of God's salvation is felt most strongly in family bonds. Family members need one another as they move toward salvation. God chose a family to reveal divine holiness. By being born into a human family, Jesus showed the world that God is involved in ordinary life. Consequently, Christian families become holy by living ordinary lives and by following Jesus' way. Families discover God's holiness whenever they manifest

God's love. In turn, young and old, rich and poor, happy and hurting families call their members to holiness. The Church supports family holiness by teaching that holiness is found in persons. Christian families become holy by loving and being loved by others. One day during my father's illness, I witnessed the kind of love that is firmly rooted in permanent bonds.

Dad was near death. Through a miracle of healing, he rallied enough to sit up in a wheelchair. I watched Mom wheel him to the window as she sat down beside him. My sister and I witnessed an epiphany of love as the sun struck our parents, illuminating their faces with a heavenly radiance. The strain resulting from a near-death agony was momentarily transformed by the intense love and joy they shared with each other. As I watched them holding hands, I knew I was on holy ground. The love they manifested went beyond human love. So did the suffering they experienced together during the long months of a struggle with illness.

To anyone walking along the hospital corridor, Mom and Dad might have appeared as two elderly people. It was their lifelong story that brought a sense of holiness to this moment. Their simple presence to each other helped me see how the holiest moments happen in the simplest ways. The divinity of a holy God is most clearly disclosed when simple people radiate an unaffected love for one another.

It made no difference that Dad's hair was uncombed or that Mom was wearing one of her older dresses. They were present to each other at the very core of their beings. Nothing else seemed to matter. A holy bond between two people goes beyond anything that a purely material existence can provide. This kind of experience reflects the kind of love Jesus demanded of his followers when he said, "This is my commandment: love one another as I loved you. No one has greater love than this, to lay down one's life for one's friends. You are my friends if you do what I command you" *(John 15:12–14)*.

Selfless love is a great family gift. By loving selflessly, Christian families discover holiness and true freedom. Family life often requires its members to live beyond themselves by giving unselfishly to other family members. I learned this lesson early in life when I met Sadie while working in my father's dry-goods store.

When I was a boy, Sadie often came into our family store to buy clothes for her children. Dad was very generous to her, often selling her clothes for less than they cost him. When she brought her children with her, their courtesy, respect, and good manners impressed me.

One day, Dad told me about Sadie. "Bob," he said, "she is a wonderful woman. Her husband left her with five small children. Ever

since then, she has worked as a maid to support them. Sadie resolved to give her life for them and to send each child through college, even if it takes all of her effort. This is the only way she feels her children will escape the wheel of poverty that has engulfed her family for generations. She never leaves those children unattended. When she works, someone watches them. On her days off, Sadie is always with her family. They'll make it, Bob, for a woman like Sadie doesn't come along every day. Her children know love from a remarkable woman."

I'll never forget Sadie or Dad's remarks. Years later, I heard that all her children went through college. In her old age, Sadie was frail and weak but happy. Her life was well spent.

The family sacramentalizes God's saving presence through selfless love. Parental sacrifice brings God's self-giving love to fulfillment. Families mature in selfless actions which reinforce mutual self-giving, ground family spirituality, and celebrate common bonds. Even when a member refuses to reciprocate, love challenges the rest of the family to give. The need to live beyond oneself is especially evident in divorce, sickness, death, or conditions of poverty. A family that imitates Jesus' self-giving symbolizes God's love.

Living beyond oneself ultimately links the family with the broader society. Community happens whenever two or more people regularly relate at the level of trust. Community, first discovered in the family, grows slowly as members reach beyond individual interests and recognize love's binding power. This happens in a unique way. Being family means laughing and crying together, being angry with one another, and ultimately forgiving one another. This give-and-take of family and community living sacramentalizes the God-with-us who gently moves people toward heaven, their final goal.

The link between family and society is important for future survival. Ancient peoples related naturally to the earth, plants, animals, and other human beings because they sensed the oneness of creation. Over the centuries, fragmentation increased in the Western world. Societies became specialized, and many people lost touch with nature's rhythms. Today's world, on the threshold of a new era of global interdependence, needs to get in touch again with the unity of all creation and the importance of human interdependence. The family is a good starting place for this to happen.

Individual use. A good follow-up activity to this question is the "Letter of Thanksgiving" activity described on page 62.

1. Describe how a holy person in your family or circle of friends helped teach you the traditions and beliefs of your faith.

2. Why do you think the Jewish people believe that people are saved together and not alone?

3. Who in your family is an example of selfless love? Describe how this person gives of himself or herself in a selfless way.

4. How do members of your family rely or depend on one another?

5. Why do you think human interdependency is essential for global survival?

Eucharist

Group use. Have a member of the group read this short section aloud while the other group members follow along in the text.

The seven sacraments, signs of God's holiness, fall into three different categories—sacraments of initiation, sacraments of healing, and sacraments of service. These sacraments revolve around the Eucharist which is at the heart of Church life.

The Eucharist needs holy families to celebrate its mystery. The Church supports family holiness by showing how God's holiness is found in persons as well as in the Eucharist. Without holy families, the Eucharist becomes a barren symbol. Without the Eucharist, holy families lack a key source of spiritual nourishment, because the Lord first dwells in people who then celebrate his dying and rising in public worship.

Christians become holy through love, and the Eucharist is about love. Because of his love for humankind, Jesus gave himself as an offering. In doing so, he freed people from the bonds of sin and bestowed on them the gift of freedom. Love and freedom are closely related. Freedom, which allows people to reach their full potential in community, reflects a love that begins with God's love and is nurtured in family relationships and the Eucharist. The Eucharist is a thanksgiving celebration for Jesus' love, poured out to gain freedom for humankind. When Christians celebrate the Eucharist, they ritualize the love and freedom that marks their existence as a holy people. I learned this lesson one Sunday while watching my small friend Scott during Mass.

As the liturgy began, Scott's four-year-old eyes greeted me with a sparkle that seemed to say, "Life is great!" At Communion time, his "give me some, too" look as he walked up the aisle with his parents, reminded me to pat his head and bless him. Then, in the church vestibule following Mass, I was greeted with "Hi! I'm Scott," to which I responded with a big hug. Finally, Scott darted back to his parents, signalling the time for his family to return home.

Scott's parents adopted him at birth and gave him a loving home and a family which also includes a sister. The love that glues this family together allows Scott to be open to others in a remarkable way for a four-year-old child. I see developing in Scott a freedom to love, revealing God's presence in his family. In many ways, the members of Scott's family are eucharistic signs to one another. When they participate in the Eucharist as a family, they receive nourishment that helps keep the power of love alive in their hearts.

Pope John Paul II calls the Eucharist the very source of Christian marriage. In *On the Family,* the Holy Father sums up the relationship between Eucharist and family life with these words:

> The eucharistic sacrifice in fact represents Christ's covenant of love with the Church, sealed with his blood on the cross. In this sacrifice of the new and eternal covenant, Christian spouses encounter the source from which their own marriage covenant flows, is interiorly structured and continuously renewed. As a representation of Christ's sacrifice of love for the Church, the Eucharist is a fountain of charity. In the eucharistic gift of charity the Christian family finds the foundation and soul of its "communion" and its "mission": By partaking in the eucharistic bread, the different members of the Christian family become one body, which reveals and shares in the wider unity of the Church *(#57).*

Group use. After you have finished reading this section, discuss these questions as a group. Then place the bread on a table and form a circle around the table. Join hands and say the Lord's Prayer together. Pass the bread around the circle. Each person, in turn, breaks a small piece from the loaf and mentions something for which he or she is thankful. After everyone has had a chance to share, all eat the bread together. Close the service either with a song everyone knows or by reciting Saint Augustine's prayer at the end of the chapter.

1. How do members of your family prepare during the week to celebrate the Eucharist?

2. How is the Eucharist a source of Christian marriage?

3. What does the celebration of Eucharist mean to your family?

4. How can members of your family become more effective eucharistic signs to one another and to the world?

Activities

Individual or group use. Choose at least one activity that is best suited to your family's life-style. Better yet, use the ideas suggested here as a springboard to create your own family activity.

All of the activities below are designed to make the ideas presented in this chapter real and concrete for your family. Because there is a variety of family situations, there is an assortment of activity suggestions. Some of the activities cater to families with small children. Others are geared toward adult reflection and participation. Feel free to adapt these suggestions to your own family needs.

Family Coat of Arms. Use poster board or butcher paper to draw a large coat of arms. Then decide as a family what symbols best describe your family. For example, a family that likes to play sports together might choose a football or baseball as one of its symbols. You can cut pictures of your chosen symbols out of magazines. Print your family name on the coat of arms and then paste or draw the family symbols around it.

Creation Walk. If you live in a rural area, near a park, or other nature spot, take a family hike or go on a picnic together. Be sure to allow enough time for family members to enjoy the wonders of creation. The point of the activity is to feel at home in the universe God created and to be thankful for all living things.

Slide Celebration. Choose a favorite family song or a reading from Scripture (for example, 1 Corinthians 13:1–13). Then create photo slides (or choose slides from your family collection) that complement the verses of the song or Scripture reading. Gather the family together and use the slide presentation as a family prayer. It would be appropriate to end the celebration with a light snack.

Home Mass. This activity is especially appropriate if a member of your family is a priest. Otherwise, even in well-populated parishes, priests often are willing to celebrate a home liturgy, especially if you gather several families together. Ask the priest to give you some guidance in choosing the readings and preparing the Mass. After the Mass is over, plan to eat together or to share some refreshments. This would be a good time to share your memories of family life.

Letter of Thanksgiving.   Recall to mind a holy person from your family or circle of friends—someone who helped you recognize God's presence in your life. Then, take some time to write a letter telling this person how much you appreciate what he or she has done for you. It is always helpful to mention specific words spoken or actions taken that were most meaningful to you. Don't forget to mail the letter!

Reflections on a Dream.   If you are married, think back to a time in late adolescence or early adulthood when you may have thought about starting a family of your own. Return to that time in your imagination and picture yourself—what you looked like, what you were doing with your life, who your friends were. Then remember what your hopes and dreams of having a family were like. What kind of family did you want? How big a family did you imagine having? What kind of spouse would you have? Then, return to the present moment and reflect on how your dream fits your current life. Was your dream realized? What parts were lost or released by you and why? Were there any surprises along the way that altered your hopes and dreams? In one or two words, how would you describe your feelings about your dream family right now? If you like, share your reflections with a spouse, relative, or friend.

Family Coupons.   Gather the family together and have each family member list five or six things he or she would like to have done for him or her. Use either construction or writing paper to make family coupons. Cut the paper into small strips and write each suggestion on a separate strip of paper. The name of the person requesting the favor should be written at the bottom of the coupon. The coupons can be posted on the family bulletin board or placed on a table where everyone can find them. During the week, each family member can take a coupon and give it to the person requesting the favor, with a promise that he or she will redeem the coupon when asked to do so.

Family Love Chain.   Take different colored sheets of construction paper and cut them into long strips. When a family member does a loving deed for another member of the family, take a strip of paper and glue the ends together to form a link in a chain. During the week, your family will watch the chain grow as the bonds of love increase.

Prayer

Through holy families, God communicates love to the world. In this prayer of Saint Augustine, Christians ask the Holy Spirit to make their lives holy.

Individual use. Consider using this prayer during the next week as your daily Morning Offering.

Breathe into me, Holy Spirit,
    that my thoughts may all be holy.
Move in me, Holy Spirit,
    that my work, too, may be holy.
Attract my heart, Holy Spirit,
    that I may love only what is holy.
Strengthen me, Holy Spirit,
    that I may defend all that is holy.
Protect me, Holy Spirit,
    that I always may be holy.

FOUR

The Family as Domestic Church

Individual use. This chapter focuses on the family as a small Church.

Group use. You will need newsprint, markers, and Bibles for this session. Begin the meeting by having someone read Philemon 1–7. Pause and allow a few moments for silent prayer. Then ask each person to share a family event that reminded him or her of God's love. Then have someone read this section aloud.

The Church sacramentalizes Jesus' life and teachings according to a particular creed and set of rituals. This sacramentality often begins in the family, where faith in the Risen Lord gives direction, meaning, and motivation to life. It is the family which first teaches Jesus' love, forgiveness, and hope. And so, the family can be described as a "domestic Church."

For many Christians, the first experience of Church is the family. Here people learn to build community, form relationships, disagree, and forgive. The broader faith community later strengthens what was learned in the home. Christ's spirit, uniquely present in each family, enables the family unit to become Church. After family members have experienced Christ's love in the home, they join other Christians in the larger Church community to profess common belief in God's love. A personal experience helped me appreciate how a family is a domestic Church.

During a visit to a rural diocese, I heard many people talk about a woman named Maria who lived in a remote area. She had a large family, but all the talk was about the long hours she spent serving the countryside's poor and needy. On my next trip to the diocese, I asked a friend of mine, who knew Maria well, to introduce me to her. He called Maria to ask her if we could visit her home. She was delighted by the request, and we were soon on our way.

Maria welcomed us into her home. I could immediately tell why this was a place where people wanted to come. We received a warm reception, something to eat, and friendship. Most of all, I was impressed by Maria's calm presence, which radiates love.

I learned why people love Maria and talk about her so often. She is a simple, earthy woman living in close friendship with her husband and family. She radiates welcome, and her spirit reflects an abiding trust in God. As we became better acquainted, Maria spoke about family joys and tragedies. She told me about her work in the neighborhood community—how she helps other people deal with life's misfortunes. Maria's family and neighborhood involvement are two forces that have helped form her faith and deepen her love of God.

Maria's family and neighbors benefit from her love—a love that gives witness to God's presence. She taught me how everyday events are opportunities to share God's love with other people. Maria, her husband, and children are a Church in miniature.

Individual use. Take a few moments to answer these questions.

1. How has faith in the Risen Christ given direction, meaning, and motivation to your life?

Group use. Allow enough time for everyone to read these questions. Then discuss your responses with one another.

2. In what ways is your family a domestic Church?

The Church on Family

Group use. Before reading this section, ask, "What is the first thing that comes to your mind when you hear the word *Church?*" If possible, list the replies on newsprint or butcher paper.

Church teaching on the family has developed gradually since the Second Vatican Council. The *Dogmatic Constitution on the Church* initiated this development by always discussing the family in the context of Church. On the topic of Christian vocation, the document states, "Incorporated into the Church by Baptism, the faithful are appointed by their baptismal character to Christian worship; reborn as sons and daughters of God, they must profess before the world the faith they have received from God through the Church" *(#11)*. By this teaching, Council members linked the individual Christian with the Church. A person first hears God's Word in a Christian community—usually the family. Then the larger Church community accepts the person as a follower of Christ through Baptism.

Strong ties exist between the larger Church community and the family. Without families, the Christian community soon loses its heart. Without Christian community, families become small private communities, and the true spirit of unity in Christ is lost. Families help the Church grow and transmit Gospel values from one generation to the next. The Church would soon die without the new life it receives from families. The Council made this clear in the *Dogmatic Constitution on the Church:*

> Christian married couples help one another to attain holiness in their married life and in their rearing of their children. Hence by reason of their state in life and of their position they have their own gifts in the people of God (cf. 1 Corinthians 7:7). From the marriage of Christians there comes the family in which new citizens of human society are born and, by the grace of the Holy Spirit in Baptism, those are made children of God so that the People of God may be perpetuated throughout the centuries *(#11)*.

Married couples receive special gifts and play an important role by virtue of their vocation. What happens in the family (beginning with two people's love) affects how family members experience God's love. The *Dogmatic Constitution on the Church* states, "In what might be regarded as the domestic Church, the parents, by word and example, are the first heralds of the faith with regard to their children" *(#11)*. Vatican II affirmed that parents are usually the first members of the Church community to speak God's Word to their children. Spouses mirror God's Word by their mutual love and the personal gifts they bring to the marriage. This love is nourished by parents, relatives, friends, and faith community. An incident from my early childhood shows how my own parents shared God's Word with me.

Just before Thanksgiving dinner, the doorbell rang. My sister Mary Ann and I ran to the door to see who was there. On the porch stood a girl about eleven years old and her younger brother. The girl carried a baby bundled in a blanket. The poorly dressed children asked for money to buy food for themselves and milk for the baby. We called our parents. Dad invited them to come inside where it was warm, but they refused. Instead, they requested money a second time.

Mom said we could not spare any money but invited them to share our Thanksgiving meal. The children gave her an odd look and refused the invitation. Then Mom offered to prepare bags of food for them, and they accepted. As Mom made turkey sandwiches from our meal, we felt very good. We were sharing our food with needy children. We returned and gave the children our gift—sandwiches, pie, dressing, and cranberries in small containers, as well as milk for the baby. They thanked us and left.

As we watched them walk away, my sister and I felt proud that we had shared our meal with such needy children. The spirit of Thanksgiving filled our hearts. But our joy soon turned to horror. The girl suddenly threw the blanketed bundle to the boy. He, in turn, tossed it over his shoulder. My sister started to cry. She thought the children had hurt the baby. I called out for Mom and Dad.

Just as our parents came outside, the children threw the food we had given them into the gutter. Laughing and joking, the children disappeared around the corner. Mary Ann and I cried and cried. But Mom explained, "Those children used a doll to trick us. They wanted money, not food. We did not know they were lying, so we gave with a generous heart. Even though the children refused our gift, it was still a true gift. Real giving comes from the heart and does not depend on the way people accept it."

Thanks to Mom's words, I learned that the value of our gift depended on our love, not on the children's response. On that Thanksgiving Day, Dad and Mom taught me more about giving than I have learned in a lifetime of reading spiritual books. My family was a miniature Church where I first learned God's love.

Pope Paul VI said,

At different moments in the Church's history and also in the Second Vatican Council, the family has well deserved the beautiful name of domestic Church. This means that there should be in every Christian family the various aspects of the entire Church. Furthermore, the family, like the Church, ought to be a place where the Gospel is transmitted and from which the Gospel radiates *(On Evangelization in the Modern World, #71)*.

Pope Paul VI carried the Council's teachings further by emphasizing that all aspects of the Church should be found in the family. In doing so, he continued the tradition of linking the larger Church community with the family. The spread of God's Word to society depends on how the Gospel radiates from Christian families.

Pope John Paul II builds on the work of his predecessors and Vatican II when he states: "Among the fundamental tasks of the Christian family is its ecclesial task: the family is placed at the service of building up the kingdom of God in history by participating in the life and mission of the Church" *(On the Family, #49).* In modern times, family and Church have the common goal of communicating God's love and teaching God's Word to the faithful. Pope John Paul II describes the family as "a living image and historical representation of the mystery of the Church" *(On the Family, #49).* As an intimate community of life and love, the Christian family is responsible for implementing the mission of the Church.

Because the family communicates God's love, Christian life demands interaction between the larger Church and the family. Through the sacraments and other rites, the Church celebrates the life already present in Christian families and helps family members grow in faith. At the same time, families who form domestic Churches share their gifts with the broader community and assist all the faithful in building the Body of Christ.

Individual use. Use these questions to broaden your understanding of the family as domestic Church.

Group use. Discuss questions 1 and 2. Then form pairs and discuss questions 3, 4, and 5. When you are finished, return to the large group and share with one another how your descriptions of Church were altered by reading this section.

1. What do you think are the key Gospel values Christians are expected to nurture?

2. Pope Paul VI said that "all aspects of the Church can be found in the family." What do these words mean to you?

3. Read Ephesians 4:1–6, 25–32. How does your family incorporate these words into its life-style?

4. As a parent, how are you a herald of faith to your children?

5. Which parish activities help you and your family understand and live the Gospel message?

Evangelization

Group use. Before beginning this section, have each person complete the sentence "Evangelization means . . ." Then silently read the entire section.

Evangelization is an ongoing process within the Christian community that seeks to call people ever more fully into the mystery of God's love manifested in the dying and rising of Jesus Christ. The term *evangelization* is misunderstood by many people. Because it is often associated with television evangelism, fundamentalist preaching, or a preliminary step to catechesis, the Catholic meaning of the term needs to be clarified. The best place to begin is with Pope Paul VI's prophetic work *On Evangelization in the Modern World.* The pope broadens the meaning of evangelization to include proclaiming God's message in word and deed. Thus, evangelization includes far more than preaching. The evangelization process goes on in the daily life of a family, at work, in social situations, and in the ordinary life of the parish.

Family, work, and Church are three chief disclosure points for evangelization. In other words, God is present in each. This approach to evangelization relates to the view of sacraments as ways of experiencing God's presence. This approach can be illustrated graphically.

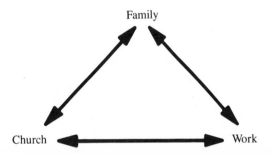

Family, work, and Church interrelate, each contributing something unique to the dialog. Evangelization (beginning in the family and spanning a lifetime) is colored by a family's life-style. And so, to understand how evangelization works in families, it helps to recognize the many different family patterns existing in today's changing world.

A family consists of two or more people, united by common bonds, who share commitment, values, and traditions. Their relationship implies permanence. This description lends itself to various family structures. Each reveals God's presence differently. The primary, or nuclear, family consists of a husband, wife, and children. Even this family type has many variations. The conventional family pattern—a mother remaining at home with the children, and a father going to work—is now in the minority. It is being replaced by the two-income family in which both husband and wife work outside of the home. The life-style of the conventional nuclear family differs from that of the two-income primary family. As two-income families become more commonplace, changes in role sharing, child rearing, and relationships occur. These changes greatly influence family faith and spirituality.

Many couples have no children of their own and do not adopt. The way God is revealed in childless families differs from how God is revealed in families with children. Another type of family—the single-parent family—has also become more common over the past few decades.

The national rise in divorces and teenage pregnancies accounts for one type of single-parent family. Others result from a separation or death in the family. Each single-parent household manifests special gifts, specific needs, and different challenges. Yet, God is present in each of these family patterns.

The rising rate of second or third marriages in the United States also contributes to the diversity in family patterns. Many blended families consist of a husband, wife, and children from one or more previous marriages. Traditionally, these families have been called stepfamilies. With a growing trend to grant joint custody in divorce cases, relationships in blended families become more and more complicated. Until relationships are firmly established and redefined, blending one or more families together can be stressful. In such diversity, the ways God reveals love and possibilities for evangelization are endless.

As a result of new family structures created by divorce and remarriage, the patterns of extended families also shift. Traditionally, extended families consisted of the primary family along with grandparents, aunts

and uncles, cousins, and other relatives. Some cultures pride themselves on the close bonds existing among extended family members. Today, extended families include ex-spouses, new spouses, stepsiblings, and assorted grandparents. The number of possible relationships within such families is limitless. And yet, faith and God's presence are very much a part of such family settings.

As more people delay marriage or choose to remain single, the informal family is emerging. These freely bonded families include specially chosen friends who are not united by either blood ties or adoption. Their responsibilities to one another are based on common values and traditions. One traditional example of a freely bonded family is the vowed religious community. Each religious order has a special charism, a history, shared values, and responsibilities to its members.

In any family pattern, the quality of relationships determines the family's health. The quality of marriage also significantly influences the quality of family life. Just because a family is intact is no guarantee it is alive and vibrant. The same applies, in reverse, to divorced and remarried families. Just because family members experience separation and divorce does not imply they are unhealthy. Basically, the health of relationships in a family will determine how members experience God's love. A happy family reflects God's presence differently from a conflict-ridden one.

Each family type has the potential to become a pilgrim people, a family-on-the-move, ever-changing, and growing in faith. Although all families can improve relationships among their members, God is present in all families—primary families, single-parent households, childless couples, blended families, extended families, and freely bonded families. Evangelizing a family does not mean bringing an absent God to the family, but rather helping that family experience more fully a God already present.

Individual use. Ask other family members to answer this question. Then compare your responses.

1. Write the names of people you consider to be members of your family. What values and traditions do you share in common?

Group use. Begin by sharing how your understanding of evangelization was altered by reading this section. Choose one or two items to discuss as a group.

2. Which family pattern best describes your family?

3. How have you experienced God in this family pattern?

4. How have you heard God speak to you through an event in your family?

Group use. Use newsprint to record your responses. Then take a break.

5. Make a list of the various kinds of family in your parish community or neighborhood. Next to each one, jot down a few words describing what you consider to be its assets and its challenges.

The Evangelizing Family

Group use. After the break, take a few minutes to read this long but important section.

The call to God's love finds its roots in family life. And so, the evangelization process starts there. In the process of evangelization, one hears of "subjects" and "objects." The expression *subject of evangelization* refers to "those who evangelize." The *object of evangelization* refers to "those who are evangelized." In practice, however, the division between subject and object is somewhat artificial. The subject of evangelization (that is, the evangelizer) is, in turn, evangelized by the object of evangelization. For example, when a person evangelizes a homeless person by providing food and shelter, he or she is also evangelized in the process. By accepting love and sharing his or her giftedness, the homeless person communicates God's love. The experience of a friend of mine demonstrates this reality.

A few years ago, my friend organized a soup kitchen to feed the homeless. What a great opportunity to evangelize! There he met Hank. Hank is not much to look at. He is bearded, broken, battered, smelly, and quite frightening. Everything he owns, he carries with him. He can't remember when he last slept in a bed. He wanders everywhere with three scruffy dogs who provide him with shelter, warmth, protection, and family. Hank is kind, talkative, and entertaining when he is sober. But he is bitter and threatening or overly religious (praising and blessing the Lord) when he is drunk.

After getting to know Hank over several bowls of hot soup, my friend noticed a change in him, or more precisely, he noticed a change in himself. His first perception of Hank was colored by fear and even loathing. He did not want to know that people like Hank exist.

One day, after a biting cold spell, my friend read that a derelict, who fit Hank's description, had been found frozen to death on a park bench. My friend became preoccupied with the man's fate. He was sure that the dead man was Hank. But when he drove up to the soup kitchen the next Saturday, there was Hank—dogs and all. When someone offered Hank some blankets, he said, "Give them to someone else. I'm too tough to freeze!" Hank felt he had more than enough warmth and protection. Someone else might need the blankets more than he did. My friend returned home that afternoon, contemplating his own life-style. Because of Hank, my friend may never have to ask the dumbest of all questions: "Lord, when did I see you hungry?"

This story demonstrates how the subject and object of evangelization always interconnect. A distinction exists only when someone needs or wants to concentrate on one aspect of the process. So, the question arises, "Is the family primarily the *subject* or the *object* of Christian evangelization?" Often professional Church leaders look upon families as the objects of evangelization. Unfortunately, this one-sided approach does not recognize clearly the reality of God's presence as it already exists in the family. A story can clarify this point.

Emma and Fred had a large family, including twelve grandchildren who loved them dearly. Fred died suddenly. And Emma was heartbroken. At the wake, Emma rose above her grief to help her grandchildren cope with their loss. Before the other adults arrived, she took the children to the casket and talked to them about their grandfather. She answered their questions, listened to their concerns, led them in prayer, and allowed each child to touch Grandpa's body. The little ones, deeply grieved by their grandfather's death, were consoled by their grandmother's love. In a real way, Emma allowed God's presence to shine through her in this moment of tragedy.

A year later, one of Emma's sons died. At the wake, his little children at first just stood around. No one paid much attention to them. The adults grieved, consoled one another, and tended to the details of the wake. Grandma Emma had not yet arrived. Finally one child said, "Let's go see Dad." This child led the other children to the casket. As the children remembered the lesson their grandmother taught, they told stories about their father, answered one another's questions, prayed together, and consoled one another. The adults looked on in amazement. Finally, the children faded back into the community.

This story shows that evangelization is a mutual activity. Emma's care for her grandchildren showed God's love and concern for them. This concern became a model for the children to imitate. In turn, the children revealed God's presence to one another and to adult family members when tragedy struck again. No priest or deacon could have pointed out God's presence more powerfully than the children did. The loving words and gestures of these family members communicated what Paul reminded the Corinthians long ago: "Death is swallowed up in victory" *(1 Corinthians 15:54)*. As God worked through the loving actions of the children, the sting of death was softened.

Evangelization takes place whenever God breaks into human experience with love and concern. And so, Church leaders regard the family as the primary *subject* of evangelization. Family becomes an *object* of evangelization only when the larger community first recognizes God's presence there. Then the larger community helps the family recognize and specify this presence. To acknowledge the family as the subject of evangelization celebrates God's incarnation. That incarnation began with creation—especially the creation of human life—and was brought to fulfillment in the person of Jesus Christ. God's incarnation continues in the evangelizing families who make up the Church.

This incarnation broadens in the shared life of community. The Church shares its values with the family and calls families to a new awareness of Jesus' presence. The larger Church must remember, however, that life itself bestows certain basic human gifts. The Church exists to celebrate these gifts, not change them, and to proclaim God's living Word to people who are already gifted. The Church supports family traditions and can never force people into an idealized model of what a Christian family should be. There are many different ways of being a holy family and manifesting God's presence in the world. In its own characteristic way, each family shows that God is truly alive in today's world. The Christian community is challenged to help families recognize their gifts. This recognition also happens in many ways.

Recently, Sally described a conversation with Barbara whose father died last summer. He was ninety-five years old. Barbara told Sally, "About three years ago, I returned home from Mass and told my dad about the homily. In his talk, Father Hater said that Christians can bless

one another and that parents especially should bless other family members. Dad seemed to take the news in stride. As I left, he blessed me. From that day, he regularly blessed his children, grandchildren, and great-grandchildren. Shortly before Dad died, we gathered around him. He spoke to each of us separately. He blessed each one individually. Then Dad gave the whole family his final blessing. I have no memory more powerful than the image of Dad's final blessing—giving us his peace and God's peace."

My homily, an action of the broader community, inspired Barbara's father to symbolize God's holiness, love, and peace by blessing his family. His act of evangelization remains forever a treasure in a family aware of God's holiness.

The Church lends support to the happy family and expresses grateful thanks for what this family gives to the community. Evangelization happens quite naturally in a happy family. In this atmosphere, people play, pray, and work together. They sense God's abiding love as they reach out to one another and to needy people.

The Church offers hope and encouragement to the hurting family. God is present in families riddled with tension—where families whose members rarely communicate with one another. Hard times provide opportunities to experience God's compassion. The key to recognizing God's love during bad times depends on whether people view God as a helper or as a punisher.

When families evangelize in these hurting times, they also resemble the Holy Family. This point came home to me during my father's illness. I heard God speak through the love shared between my father and his grandchildren. Whenever possible, Dad wanted to be with his grandchildren. He needed their love. They needed his care. Dad's approaching death affected Julie and Joe most of all.

Five-year-old Julie showed me the wisdom of letting a child experience family joy and grief. One day Julie said she was glad she saw her grandpa three times in the hospital. When I asked her why, she replied, "Because Grandpa might die soon. When he does, Jesus will call him back to himself." It will be easier for Julie to cope with death than it is for children who do not know the reality of suffering.

Dad's sickness also profoundly affected sixteen-year-old Joe. Dad was his inspiration and hero. One afternoon, when Dad was very weak, Joe walked out of the hospital room, crying. He said, "Grandpa is lucky. Pretty soon, he will be with God. Grandpa is so sure of himself. I wish I were as sure about myself." Dad's sickness influenced Joe. He learned fundamental life values during his grandfather's final illness.

Evangelization happened very naturally in my father's relationship with the children. During his illness, our family learned why Jesus said the reign of God belongs to children and to those who become like children. We all discovered the power of God's love in our family suffering. Our mutual support was a powerful evangelizing influence. We were called by life itself, by faith in God and in one another, and by the help of friends. We celebrated in prayer and in Eucharist the beauty and pain we experienced as a family.

The evangelization process continues in our family. We share what we have learned with God's broader family. Watching my family respond to Dad's illness and subsequent death reaffirmed for me that God is present in every family. When the Church evangelizes a family (as the *object),* God's presence in each family (the *subject)* must be recognized. Otherwise, Church efforts may never meet real family needs.

Individual use. Use these questions to explore how family members evangelize one another.

1. Which members of your family have helped you experience God's love? How?

2. Recall an evangelizing event in your family. What happened and how did your family experience God in this event?

Individual or group use. Parish leaders might be interested in hearing your suggestions.

3. How can the Church better help you find God within your family?

The Family and Work

Group use. If there is not enough time to read this section during the meeting, read it at home. Instead, discuss questions 3, 4, and 5 at the end of this section.

Work or human labor is the second disclosure point of evangelization. By their work, family members reveal God to the broader society. Pope John Paul II's encyclical *On Human Work* sees work as fulfilling two functions: *(1)* It serves immediate family needs, and *(2)* it spreads God's message to the world. The Holy Father uses the term *work* or *labor* to include physical, intellectual, and spiritual activities. Work is a person's proper vocation. By his or her work, an individual "created in the image of God shares . . . in the activity of the Creator; and that, within the limits of one's capabilities, a person in a sense continues to develop that activity" *(On Human Work, #10)*. Work is the way to "proclaim the Gospel to all people," for it is "a foundation for the formation of family life" *(On Human Work, #10)*. Whenever work is rooted in love, the family moves through it to God.

Healthy families recognize dependence on the world and responsibility for it. In this relationship, they acknowledge obligations to the Church community, neighbors, city, country, earth, and universe. By nurturing Gospel values at home, Christian families are more likely to carry these same values into the world. Then they are helping to evangelize society. During Pope John Paul II's second pastoral visit to the United States, Archbishop Rembert Weakland offered several challenges to the Church. One of those challenges focused on work. According to Archbishop Weakland, laypeople are asking the Church to help them bring Gospel values to their work, to society, and to the political arena. Laypeople sense a dichotomy between their private lives and their public commitments. So, laypeople are searching for a spirituality that integrates their family, work, and social responsibilities—a spirituality that does not condemn the technological world in which they live and work. They sense the tensions between work and family responsibilities, and expect their faith to integrate these demands with Gospel imperatives.

Work situations vary. The work of youth revolves around school. Students reflect Christian values by the way they relate to other students, by how hard they study, and by their honesty and integrity. As they mature intellectually, young people can relate what they learn in school to their faith.

Christian teachers reflect Gospel values by their attitudes toward students and colleagues. They also share these values by the way they prepare lessons and teach classes. Gloria teaches Spanish in a public high school and volunteers as a catechist in her parish religious education program. She told a pastoral minister that she wanted to teach in the Catholic school system, but as her family's sole provider, she could not afford to take a salary cut. Gloria often wanted to talk about her faith to her language students, but this could not happen in a public school setting.

Gloria related how she once helped a young student. The fifteen-year-old girl was pregnant. Her boyfriend pressed her to get an abortion,

but the girl didn't feel right about it. She confided in Gloria who was her favorite teacher. The girl worried that her parents would be angry with her for getting pregnant. Gloria offered to go with the girl when she told her parents. The girl's concern was well founded. Her enraged parents demanded that she get an abortion. Gloria asked the parents to calm down and think about the situation. Gloria offered to take the girl home for a few days. Over the next several weeks, Gloria acted as a healing catalyst. She directed the hurting family to a counselor and helped the parents support their daughter's decision to have the baby. Gloria continued to provide emotional support to the family throughout the pregnancy. After the delivery, when the girl put the baby up for adoption, Gloria was there for that family.

Gloria may not have been allowed to talk openly in the classroom about her faith, but her caring attitude spoke volumes. Through Gloria, Christ's healing power touched a family in crisis. No matter where a person works, there are many opportunities to evangelize by word or by action.

Besides bringing God's love to the world through their work or professions, Christians also assist the Church by using their skills and talents. Gloria taught in the parish religious education program. Others serve on finance committees, are eucharistic ministers or lectors, care for the sick, visit jails, paint the parish hall, help people fill out tax forms or immigration papers, bake cookies for the parish carnival, work with youth, and so on. Archbishop Weakland, in his address to the Holy Father, pointed to the many Christians with professional competencies who help solve today's most complicated social issues—especially bioethics and the economy. This reality demands a new kind of collaboration and a consultation on the part of the Church—a new definition of ministry.

The Church, a third disclosure point of the evangelization process, takes an interest in human work and its relationship to family life. During the nineteenth century, Pope Leo XIII's encyclical *Rerum Novarum,* "On the Condition of the Working Man," addressed issues relating to the government's role in society and in the economy, the laborer's right to organize, the principle of a just wage, and a Christian critique of capitalism and socialism. After Vatican II, Church teaching has focused on the international dimensions of social doctrine. The Church challenges Catholics to share in the political life of the community at the local, national, and international levels. Catholics are to champion the cause of human rights for all peoples. The Church asks families to show concern for the human family by using their gifts, skills, and talents to build a more just society. Each family does this in a different way. The sense of justice develops in the family in the way members treat one another. From the just family, justice radiates into the neighborhood, parish, nation, and world. Christian families are at the center of the contemporary search for meaning. Through physical, intellectual, and spiritual work, families carry God's love into the world and help society discover life's purpose.

Individual use. Many psychologists claim that an emotionally healthy person knows how to do two things—love and work. Use these questions to ponder the meaning and place of work in your life.

1. Read Matthew 19:16–22 and compare it with Luke 18:18–23. The stories' main characters are both rich when they come into contact with Jesus. The two men respond to Jesus' invitation in very different ways. How does contact with Jesus affect each person? Are you more like the rich man or Zacchaeus? If you feel comfortable doing so, explain your answer.

2. Read Luke 15:8–10. How does the woman in this story approach her work?

3. What work do you do?

4. How do you reflect Gospel values in your work?

5. How do family responsibilities and work conflict in your family?

Activities

These suggested activities can help your family discover God's presence already at work within the family. Some of the activities focus on evangelizing ministry within the family. Others concentrate on the family's evangelizing role in the world. Some of the activities encourage total family participation, and others can be done alone or with one or more people.

Group use. Before you end the meeting, quickly review the activities in this section. See if anyone wants to offer additional suggestions. Then close the meeting with either a traditional prayer, like the Our Father, or a spontaneous prayer.

Individual use. Before going to the next chapter, choose an activity that reflects your family's current needs and do it with them.

A Holy Symbol. Buy a candle or designate a special cup as the family's holy symbol. At mealtime or at some other appropriate moment, explain to your family that this symbol will be used on special occasions as a reminder that God is present in the family. If you choose a candle, tell the family it will be lit during times of danger or when someone is sick or hurt. If you choose a cup, tell the family members it will be used only during special family events—like Christmas, Easter, First Holy Communion, wedding anniversaries, birthday parties, and the like.

A Family Calendar. Make a large-sized calendar for a one-month period. You might want to design it in the shape of a church and write in Scripture references for each day. Make the spaces large enough for family members to record information in them. Refer to the calendar at dinnertime or at any time all family members are gathered together. Invite family members to use the calendar to keep track of the family's good deeds as well as the schedule of events. No one should record his or her own good deeds, only those of other family members. The idea is for the family to notice how God shines through family relationships and life.

Reflections on a Marriage or Family. With your spouse or other family members, consider two marriages or families that you know well and discuss how each divides responsibilities like child rearing, earning a living, household chores, and family activities. Then discuss your own marriage or family life and how you handle these and other responsibilities. Describe changes that have taken place over the years and how your family handled the changes. Talk honestly about changes you want to make in the future. Discuss how these changes could affect the whole family.

Welcome to the Family. Have the family make a picture to hang on the entrance door to your home. Include a saying like "God Bless This Home" or "Welcome to Our Home." Decorate the picture with symbols that capture the essence of your family life. If your family knows how to make a découpage, you can make the picture a family plaque.

Volunteering.   Decide how to use your family skills in service to your parish or neighborhood community. Be specific and follow through.

Gaining Knowledge.   From your parish library, a local library, or a religious bookstore, obtain a copy of an encyclical or a pastoral letter on family or labor. Read and discuss the document with a friend or relative. Look for Pope John Paul II's *On the Family* or *On Human Work,* Pope Paul VI's *On Evangelization in the Modern World* or *The Progress of Peoples,* Pope John XXIII's *Peace on Earth,* and the United States Bishops' pastoral letter *Economic Justice for All.*

Home Blessing.   Make a copy of the home blessing *(see* the "Prayer" section) for each family member. Choose a time when all family members can gather together to bless the home. Begin in the living room or the family room and invite family members to recall special events that occurred there. When everyone is finished reminiscing, read the home blessing prayer together before going to the next room. Follow the same procedure for each room until you have blessed the whole house.

Family Work Day.   On a day when all family members are free, gather together early in the morning. Make a list of the chores that need to be done around the house and decide how family members can team up to complete the work. Break for a special lunch. Give thanks for the food and for your labor. If more work needs to be done, continue into the afternoon until you are finished. Try to plan some fun for the evening, so that everyone can relax after a hard day's work.

Prayer

A parish church symbolizes the Church as the People of God. In a similar fashion, the home symbolizes the family that lives there. Each home has a specific atmosphere—a spirit which pervades the family. And God is in the home—at the heart of family life. The following prayer is a home blessing. Use it with your family to celebrate this divine presence.

Individual or group use. This prayer works well with the "Home Blessing" activity.

Holy God, our Creator and loving parent,
To you, we dedicate this home and all that is in it.
Bless our family, our household, and all who enter here.
Make each room holy, and each person a sign of your love.
Fill this house with your blessings,
As you filled the house of Nazareth with your presence.
Amen.

FIVE

Sources of Family Growth

Individual use. This chapter shows how families are organized and grow in faith.

Group use. You will need a large ball of yarn for this activity. Hold the ball in both hands and give a brief description of yourself. Then hold on to the end of the yarn and throw the ball to someone else. The process is repeated until everyone is wrapped in yarn. Afterward, take turns reading this section aloud.

A priest once told me how his family learned faith and hope through mutual love and trust. "When I was nine," he began, "Dad called me into his room, opened a small box containing important papers, and took out a handful of documents. Holding two of them, he said, 'Jake, this paper was worth ten thousand dollars! This one four thousand!' Then he tore them up and continued, 'Altogether these papers were worth eighty thousand dollars.' When I asked him why he destroyed them, my father replied, 'The other day the banks failed. Now the papers are worthless. We have no money.'

"I was shocked. My father continued, 'Don't worry, son, we have five million dollars.' I asked, 'Where is the five million, Dad?' He smiled and said, 'Jake, you are one million, and your brother, sister, Mom, and I are the other four million dollars. With God's help, we will make it together.'"

The priest's story is reminiscent of the Holy Family. God's presence in the Holy Family gives all Christian families hope. Scripture presents the Holy Family as hope-filled, yet broken. Matthew and Luke both describe the family's unity in the midst of pain, doubt, and uncertainty. From the Holy Family, Christians learn how love, truth, justice, and forgiveness help families survive hard times.

Before Vatican II, the Church frequently used the Holy Family as the model of a perfect family. This idealistic picture, combined with emphasis on Jesus' divinity, differed from the synoptic Gospels' portrait of a real, human family. New insights into Gospel stories of the Holy Family and a greater appreciation of Jesus' humanity have invited Christians to reappraise this image.

The Church is not calling on families to measure up to Jesus, Mary, and Joseph. Rather, the sweat and tears of the Holy Family are sources of hope for the real needs of today's families. Christians are called to minister to people's brokenness and to support them through painful times. Outreach to the divorced, to families struggling with sick members, to abandoned children, to people needing counseling, and to chemically dependent family members brings more hope to a community than an icon of family perfection.

Reaching out to hurting families helps Christians examine their priorities. Until recently, the Church did little for divorced or blended families. When this Church attitude changed, the results were startling. This was evident at the first meeting of an outreach program for separated and divorced Catholics.

The body language in the room showed the unusual nature of the gathering. People fidgeted. Many sat on the edge of their chairs. But the moment the keynote speaker proclaimed the Church's desire to help, people began to settle back and relax.

During the intermission, I asked a divorced man how he felt about the meeting. "Great," he responded. "Didn't you notice what happened shortly after we started? We began to unwind. The Church really wants to help us. It's been years in coming. I feel reborn as a Catholic."

For many years, the Church neglected divorced people. In some Catholic families, divorce was the big family secret. In addition to feeling lost, divorced people often experienced shame and guilt. The Church's attitude toward the divorced made them feel like outcasts.

Christian communities that neglect hurting families may be guilty of collective sin. Instead of forcing the suffering families to the margins of the community, Christians need to welcome these people in pain, especially the divorced and separated. In doing so, Christians reveal God's compassion.

Of course, the Church must never forget happy families. Happy people are special signs of God's love who require affirmation. The descriptions *happy* and *hurting* are not static terms. Most families go through cycles which mingle happiness and pain. Christian communities provide hope when happy and hurting families are encouraged to come together to give support to one another.

Jim worked on a construction site near a railroad bridge which spanned a large river. Often he saw a beggar disappear beneath the metal structures. One day, Jim discovered that the man and his son lived there in an abandoned shack. As the months passed, the two men became friends. So, Jim's family decided to give the poor man's family something for Christmas.

On Christmas Eve, Jim, his wife Elaine, and their children all came to the shack. They were bringing the man a new coat and his son a pair of pants, a sweater, and a shirt. Jim knocked on the dilapidated door. Embarrassed, yet happy, the beggar man and his son welcomed Jim's family into their one-room house. The clothes fit the son, but the jacket was too large for the father. Disappointment showed on Jim's face, but the poor man said, "Please don't return it. I want to keep it. The Lord will bless you." Jim said, "God has already blessed us. Your love has taught us much this Christmas."

Christians learn about families by appreciating patterns common to all families. All families share similar characteristics and concerns which root the differences that make them unique. Every family is incomplete, but each one is on the move toward wholeness. Circumstances may differ, but every family needs peace, love, and trust. At some point, all families experience pain, disappointment, and failure. Christian hope springs from a belief in God's presence during life's high and low points. In the struggle for wholeness, families become holy and generate holiness in others. Holy families—not perfect families—are sources of hope in dark and painful times.

Individual use. Some of these questions are personal. Others refer to the parish. You might bring some of the general issues to the attention of your pastor or parish council.

Group use. Choose any or all of these questions for group discussion.

1. In terms of time, energy, and resources, what do you think are your parish's priorities?

2. Which groups of people or family types do you think are most neglected by the Church today?

3. What is your attitude toward separation and divorce?

4. How does your family deal with pain and brokenness?

5. What kind of affirmation does your family most need from the Church?

6. How does a holy family differ from a perfect family?

A Living System

Group use. Begin by asking someone to read the first four paragraphs of this section.

Christian faith and hope give a family roots. The family is a living and growing system which evolves through intricate interpersonal relationships. As a unit, the family is more complex than the sum of its individual members. In this network of relationships, changes affecting one family member affect the entire family. As a family grows, complex and sometimes unconscious patterns develop. Recognizing these patterns is not easy. When these patterns are identified, they pinpoint family strengths or trouble spots. This became clear to me one day while I was speaking with a mother and her two daughters.

Donna asked me to meet with her two teenagers, Maggie and Paula, who were always fighting. The mother claimed that Maggie— the younger girl—caused the trouble. I asked Donna to come with her daughters.

When the family arrived, Paula sat next to her mother. Maggie sat to the side. This pattern continued every time I saw them. Gradually, I realized the mother's affection chiefly focused on the older child. The real issue was not the girls' fighting but Maggie's resentment toward her mother who favored Paula.

Donna asked me to see her daughters, unaware that she was the source of the problem. One person's actions affect other family members. A change in this member's behavior tends to produce corresponding changes in other members. When Donna saw how her favoritism affected Maggie, she changed her behavior. In turn, Maggie and Paula's relationship improved.

When considering the family as a system, it is easy to see how important community is. People do not prosper in a vacuum. To grow and develop, people need relationships. As children mature, they move beyond their families, not for isolated independence, but for other human systems. The need for community continues throughout a person's lifetime, and people require interpersonal skills to adapt to new relationships. The family, a training ground for developing human relationships, teaches people how to live happy lives.

The Apostle Paul, recognizing the importance of relationships, described the Church as Christ's Body. Much can be learned about family

Group use. Before proceeding with the text, pause here and discuss similar situations you and your family have experienced. Then have a group member read the rest of the section aloud.

systems and how they work by reading what Saint Paul wrote to the Corinthians:

> But as it is, God placed the parts, each one of them, in the body as he intended. If they were all one part, where would the body be? But as it is, there are many parts, yet one body. The eye cannot say to the hand, "I do not need you," nor again the head to the feet, "I do not need you." Indeed, the parts of the body that seem to be weaker are all the more necessary, and those parts of the body that we consider less honorable we surround with greater honor, and our less presentable parts are treated with greater propriety, whereas our more presentable parts do not need this. But God has so constructed the body as to give greater honor to a part that is without it, so that there may be no division in the body, but that the parts may have the same concern for one another. If one part suffers, all the parts suffer with it; if one part is honored, all the parts share its joy *(1 Corinthians 12:18–26)*.

Individual family members continually influence, and are influenced by, one another. Family struggles often revolve around conflicts between individual rights and family needs, values, and traditions. Thriving families recognize the interplay between family unity and individual growth. Holy families realize that the whole family must pull together for its individual members to prosper. This principle applies to both happy and hurting families. Family unity and individual growth are sources of hope.

Group use. Choose a partner to discuss questions 1 and 2. Then write your response to item 3 and share it with the large group.

1. Think about a specific change (for example, a job change, someone moving out of the house, separation or divorce, sickness, a change in financial status, or the like) that has occurred in your family. How did this change affect each family member?

2. Recall a specific occasion when an individual's need or behavior conflicted with family traditions or values. How did the family as a whole and each member individually handle the situation?

Individual use. Consider using this item as the basis of a family activity or sharing session.

3. Consider the human body and each of its members. Write down each family member's name and, next to it, describe what part of the body that person is like. (For example, "John is like a hand because he fixes things around the house.")

Family Growth

Group use. This section deals with family growth through conflict. Take turns reading this section aloud.

When a man and a woman marry, they promise fidelity to each other in good and bad times. Jesus required this kind of faith when he asked his disciples to leave everything and follow him. For married people to follow Jesus, they must place top priority on family relationships and on allowing the Spirit of Christ to motivate family life. This Spirit gives courage to families suffering from misunderstandings, sickness, or death. When married love grows through joy, suffering, conflict, and reconciliation, a couple is building a solid foundation for lasting fidelity.

Love and concern for each other is the greatest gift parents can give their children. As the couple's love grows, children instinctively grow to appreciate their father and mother. When spousal love wavers or when parents compete for sibling affection, other problems surface in the family system. A lack of significant interpersonal communication between husband and wife blocks growth. This occurs whenever spouses continually blame each other, harbor unspoken grudges, or fail to communicate on any but a superficial level. Movement toward wholeness requires open communication between spouses.

No spousal relationship is perfect. Today, an increasing number of husbands and wives divorce or abandon their families because of unresolved conflict. Sometimes the conflict really is unresolvable. Sometimes only one party wants to work it out. Sometimes spouses separate to relieve a painful relationship. Often, however, separation can be avoided if the couple realizes that conflict itself can lead to growth. Conflict alone is not a sufficient reason to break up a family.

Serious disagreements are not always signs of incompatibility. Since the struggle to become whole involves pain, growth takes place as couples learn how to work through their problems and negotiate their disagreements. This requires a healthy respect for each other, even in the

face of differences. Negotiation involves accepting differences and working toward shared goals.

Families that value individuality encourage family members to speak up. Such families deal with conflict by relating to, rather than controlling, one another. When this happens, husband and wife or other family members take responsibility for their own thoughts, feelings, and behavior. They listen and respect different points of view. They are slow to blame or to attack other persons. Even in the midst of serious conflict, they recognize that people make mistakes.

When a sense of humor and mutual trust exist in a family, growth can take place. Conflict is part of life. If parents show successful ways of resolving conflict, children will more easily learn how to relate to people, respect differences, and resolve conflicts themselves. In this atmosphere of tolerance, family members mature with patience and respect for all.

Families can be sources of hope to today's world—a global village of races, creeds, and religions. People can accept the arsenal of nuclear warheads as the symbol of how nations relate to one another. Or people can change this symbol as they learn to resolve differences within their families. Then the world will be blessed with more peacemakers. Families attempting to resolve conflict resemble the Holy Family in the way Jesus, Mary, and Joseph confronted obstacles throughout life. Conflict resolution and family growth go hand in hand.

Individual use. These questions help you explore how your family handles conflict. Use this occasion to talk to family members about specific situations.

1. From your experiences, describe one family conflict that has been resolved. Who was involved? How did it affect other family members? How was it resolved?

Group use. Allow time for everyone to read these questions. Each member then chooses one question and shares his or her response with the group. At the end of the discussion, take a break.

2. How do you normally deal with conflict in your family?

3. When and how has a sense of humor helped you or your family survive a painful time?

The Family Life Cycle

Group use. This is an important section. After the break, take sufficient time to read it thoroughly. At the end of the section, write your responses to the questions.

The family is a living system which grows and matures over a period of time. In the family life cycle, even ordinary change can upset the family system and produce powerful emotions. How a family copes with change can propel a family forward or push them backward in the development of unity and respect.

All families go through life cycles with specific and observable stages. Each stage presents its own challenges and requires change from family members. Each stage has its own theme, mood, special problems, and turning points. These all lead to a new stage in the family's development.

Before marriage, a man and woman, drawn together by mutual love and interests, seek to learn each other's beliefs, thoughts, emotions, and values. They often spend more time with each other than with friends and family members. Wedding plans bring excitement and tension. The couple forms impressions that may last far into the marriage.

After the wedding ceremony, the couple begins to adjust to married life. Now, instead of searching for time to spend with one another, each spouse may need to discover ways to be alone. Mutually irritating habits often emerge. He forgets to turn off the television. She leaves clothes on the floor. The couple encounters a turning point in their relationship as they adjust to life together.

When children come, new challenges emerge. Having children is not like adding new furniture to a house. The birth of a child means shifting from a relationship centered on two people to one dedicated to the nurture of new life. Often, the first child brings a rude awakening. Before children come, many couples have romantic ideas about parenting. When the first child arrives, the family system changes. The baby throws the family onto a new schedule. Sleep is often interrupted. Couples spend less time with each other, a trend that continues as the child grows up.

Jack and Phyllis now have two children. They married after a long and satisfying courtship. Since they both wanted children, Phyllis's first pregnancy delighted the couple. Jack described how he changed after their first child's birth. "I was proud to be a father. I delighted in taking pictures and showing them to anyone who would look. But at home, I often got annoyed at Phyllis because she didn't give me enough attention. Our sexual relationship suffered. We were usually tired from caring for the baby. I loved my child but wanted my life to be the same as it was before he was born."

Phyllis described her experience in becoming a parent. "The delivery was long and painful, but I was delighted when I saw my son. Jack's presence at delivery time made all the difference in the world. While holding Jason in my arms, I felt God had brought the three of us together. But when we took the baby home, I no longer had time for the things I enjoyed doing. I returned to work after several weeks but missed my baby and worried about his day-care program. I felt Jack had lost interest in me, and I resented doing most of the work at home."

Jack and Phyllis eventually realized what was happening. They spoke with each other about their difficulties and recognized a mutual need to rekindle the intimacy they enjoyed during the early part of their marriage. They joined a young parents' group in their parish. From other people, they discovered new ways to juggle work, parenthood, and their relationship. They successfully made the transition into parenthood because they communicated with each other and sought other people's help.

When their second child was born, Phyllis and Jack saw more clearly the steps they needed to take to maintain family health.

The experience of becoming a parent differs for people who adopt and for people who give birth to babies with special needs. Adoptive families usually wait a long time before getting a child. Social workers or other qualified people examine their financial situation, household, emotional maturity, and ability to raise a family. This can be stressful. If the adopted child is older, there will be an adjustment period. If the child has been in one or more foster homes, a longer adjustment period may be necessary. An adopted child from a different ethnic background requires special sensitivity. Families who give birth to or adopt a child with special problems or needs face a different set of challenges.

Other stages of the family life cycle include going to school, the empty nest, becoming grandparents, retirement, the death of a spouse or a child. In some families, the cycles include separation and divorce, becoming single again, remarrying, and blending of two families. Each situation involves challenges and an opportunity for family growth. God is always present throughout the cycles. As family members mature, they integrate this divine presence into their lives and become signs of God's love.

Individual use. Write responses to the items that apply to you.

Group use. When everyone is finished writing his or her responses to these items, discuss how you have seen your family grow and change over the years.

1. Describe one transition your family made and how each family member handled it.

2. If you are married, describe your courtship period. What were the strengths and challenges you encountered during this time?

3. If you are not married, remember a time when a family member or a friend got engaged. How did your relationship with that person change? How did you respond to this change?

4. If you have children, describe what changes occurred in your life as a result of parenthood.

5. What are the major challenges parents face today?

Growth in Faith

God works through the family. But not all families or family members are on the same level of faith. Some families grow together in faith. Others seem to have no apparent faith. Still others turn to God only in crisis situations. Faith differences exist within each family as well as from family to family.

The Rite of Christian Initiation of Adults (RCIA)—a process of initiating people into the Church—stresses that faith develops in stages. The initial inquiry period may involve doubt and questioning. When a person takes the first step of becoming a catechumen, the second period begins. This period encourages growth in faith through community, instruction, and integration of the Gospel message into one's life. This period leads a person to the step of election which emphasizes enlightenment, prayer, and a deepening of faith. Election climaxes in the celebration of the sacraments of initiation during the Easter Vigil. The process does not end with the reception of the sacraments but continues in the fourth, or mystagogical, period, when the newly initiated take their place in the community.

Faith development takes place in three basic stages: *(1)* initial questioning (inquiry period), *(2)* inquiring with faith (catechumenate and enlightenment period), and *(3)* responding in communal faith (mystagogical period). Families do well to recognize these faith stages in their members. The stages are all based on people's need to question. The answers people receive to their questions will affect their spiritual journey.

During the initial questioning period, a person often signals that he or she is at a turning point in the religious quest. Questioning does not indicate a lack of faith. Rather, it most often signifies movement toward a more mature faith. The questioner, however, may not yet have made a mature decision for God, Jesus, or the Church.

A person who is inquiring with faith is ready to listen to God's Word. This implies a certain development of faith and a decision to learn more about Jesus' message and about the meaning and life of the Church. Commitment to Jesus' teaching, however, does not always imply an equal commitment to the Church's significance in one's life.

The development of a shared faith requires membership in the Church community. Even though inquiring faith can help one *see* that the Christian faith is a communal experience of Word, worship, and service, that vision is barren without active participation. Family members who are not yet fully convinced of the Church's necessity in their lives should still be encouraged to attend church activities and services. Ritualizing belief in significant ways helps people develop a communal faith.

Many young people believe in Jesus but have no deep commitment to the Church. If this is where they are, parents and others need to recognize their faith levels. Through example and encouragement, young people often begin to accept the importance of the Church. This acceptance may not be complete until later in life—perhaps not until the young people have children of their own.

Christian initiation is lifelong and reflects the stages of faith development. In any family, some members may be in the doubting stage, while others actively make the Gospel a part of their lives. Some family members need time for prayer, and others commit to active service. Throughout life, faith moves in a cyclical fashion. A person questioning God's existence one month may attend Scripture classes the next. Even people of great faith experience doubt and uncertainty. Families grow together when these differences are recognized and members communicate their individual stages of faith. Family members move toward God, even when they are on different psychological and spiritual levels. Each faith level has its own strengths and must be respected.

I remember an incident when my dad was dying. I had just left the hospital room. Dad was weak, and I felt discouraged. I met a person who said, "The Lord must really love you to let you suffer so much." Anger overcame me, and I responded, "Leave me alone. I don't want to hear of God's love. Right now, it doesn't make sense to me."

The person meant well, but I did not want any explanations at that moment. In hurting times, words often mean less than the simple expressions of another's love. Family joys and sorrows *are* experiences of Church. The simple, real human responses in the faith-filled family don't need pious words to make them holy.

The thorny issue of attendance at Sunday Eucharist can often be better handled by example and human discernment than by sermons on the value of common worship. Families need to acknowledge where members are with regard to church attendance. Some teenagers don't want to go to church because they are lazy or bored. Others are seriously struggling with faith. Parents should consider all the circumstances before deciding whether or not to force children to go to Mass. This issue and others like it can allow parents and children to dialog about matters of faith and Catholic practice.

It is important to remember that God's presence is not limited to formal religious experiences. This simple truth came home to me one day while I was repairing my car.

I had just finished fixing my car when two small girls approached me. They came from one of those faceless families that appear and disappear in any poor, transient neighborhood. "Hi, Mister, have you seen our brother? He's hiding," they began. Their faces were dirty, and their clothes were ragged and torn. But through the dirt, I saw their beautiful, longing eyes.

"What are your names?" I asked.

"I'm Sadie and she's Amy" was the response.

We talked for some time. Then seven-year-old Sadie asked, "Mister, are you a Christian?"

Surprised by the inquiry, I responded, "Yes." In turn, I asked, "Are you Christians?"

"Oh, no," Sadie exclaimed. "Mom won't let us be Christians."

As she answered, six-year-old Amy shook her head and repeated, "Our mom won't let us pray or even mention Jesus."

I ended our theological conversation by saying, "Maybe you can become Christians when you grow up."

As they walked away, I heard Sadie telling Amy, "When I get big, I want to be a Christian like that man."

Amy answered, "Me, too."

God lives in Sadie and Amy, even though religious practices are absent in their home. They feel God's love through life itself—through nature, family, and good people. God works through all life, and in a special way, family relationships clarify, deepen, and give meaning to God's presence.

Individual use. These questions help you see how faith has developed in your family.

1. What life events have helped you and your family grow in faith?

Group use. Either use these questions for group discussion or use "The Emmaus Story" in the "Activities" section.

2. Consider several aspects of faith development: doubting, learning, praying, and serving. Which is most significant for you now?

3. Is there an event in Jesus' life that reminds you of aspects of your own faith journey? Why so?

4. At what stage of faith development do you discern each member of your family to be?

5. How does an awareness of differing stages, or levels, of faith help you better understand family members?

Activities

Individual and group use. Read the activity suggestions listed here and decide which one you want to use with your family. Feel free to create your own or to alter one of these activities to meet your family's needs.

Families are sources of hope when members learn how to grow through conflict, listen to and communicate openly with each other, respect differences, share in life's happenings, and work together for the growth of each individual and the family as a whole. The following activities can help families develop these skills.

Planting a Seed.   This activity works especially well in families with small children. Take a flower pot, some soil, and flower seeds or a bulb. As a family, plant the seeds or bulb and discuss with your child what the plant needs to grow. Over the weeks, as the plant begins to grow, discuss how your family is like the plant. Talk about what each family member needs to grow and what happens when these things are (or are not) present in the family.

Rekindling the Flame.   This activity works well with couples with children, childless couples who have demanding jobs or other responsibilities, and older couples. As a couple, plan how both of you can find a specific time to spend alone with each other. This may involve saving money to hire a babysitter, getting members of the extended family to help out, or rearranging your business calendars. Decide what you would like to do and plan the occasion. Be as specific as possible. Write the date on your calendar, and take the necessary steps to make sure you keep your date.

From Generation to Generation.   This activity works well with all families, including extended families with grandparents. Make a scrapbook or a tape recording which documents the family history. (Families that have video recording equipment might choose to videotape the session.) If you make a scrapbook, use pictures and stories of how the grandparents met, their early married years, their work, special activities, and so forth. Then show how their children grew up and the major events in the family's life. This project can involve the entire family. (Be aware that this is a long project.)

The tape-recording idea works best with older family members. Begin the project by asking the family elders for an interview. Explain that you want to record family memories so that future generations will know their family history. Decide what you want to know about your early family history and prepare specific questions. If you have children, involve them in the project. On the day of the interview, be sure to choose a comfortable place to record and to have refreshments available. Allow the person being interviewed to add his or her own comments after you complete the questions.

Family Skit. This activity works well with families that like to playact. If family members have a healthy respect for one another, this activity can provide meaningful insight into family communication patterns. If, however, your family is going through a difficult period or certain family members are particularly sensitive, this activity may not be a good choice right now. Families should consider the effects before choosing this activity.

When the family is gathered together, exchange roles with one another. In other words, one child can play mother, the mother takes the role of a child, and so forth. Choose a typical family scenario—a mealtime conversation, selecting television shows, or planning a family outing. Explain that everyone is to act the way he or she thinks the character would act. Since there is no script, everyone ad libs. Begin the little play and let it proceed for about five or ten minutes. Be sure to keep it light and fun. When you are finished, discuss how accurate or inaccurate the role-playing was. If someone gets angry at the way he or she was portrayed, allow this person to express these feelings in an appropriate way. Later on, spend some personal time with the hurting individual, discussing the situation. If the portrayal was inaccurate, it would be good to involve the actor to get to the root of the problem. If the portrayal seemed to be correct, help the individual recognize and work on any weakness. Be sure to take a good look at how the parents were portrayed.

The Emmaus Story. This activity can be done alone or with other family members. Read Luke 24:13–35. This Scripture story reflects how an individual's faith grows and develops. Note each movement in the story: *(a)* the disciples' discouragement and inability to recognize the Lord who is with them, *(b)* the women's excitement and hope as they report their vision, *(c)* the disciples' discovery that Scripture is the living

Word of God, *(d)* their recognizing and experiencing the Risen Lord in the breaking of the bread, and *(e)* their going forth to spread the Good News. If you do this activity with other people, share which movement of the story parallels your faith journey at this moment. Describe what is happening in your life and relate how this passage might help you grow in faith. If you do this activity alone, write your feelings and thoughts in a notebook or journal. You may expand the activity by sharing or writing about other times you experienced a development in faith.

Separation and Divorce. If you are recently separated or divorced, find out what support programs your parish or diocese offers. Good sources of information include your parish priests or director of religious education, the diocesan family life office, and the diocesan newspaper. Parish leaders can give you the names and phone numbers of diocesan personnel who might know of programs if none exist in your parish. You might even consider starting a support group. If you want to explore the possibility of an annulment but have lots of questions, make an appointment with a trusted priest or deacon who can help you.

Prayer

On March 25, 1987, Pope John Paul II asked the Catholic world to observe a Marian Year in honor of Mary, the Mother of God. At this time, the pope entrusted the world to Mary in the following prayer. Christian families, hopeful sources of world peace, can use this prayer at home.

Individual use. During the next week, consider using this prayer as an evening prayer.

Group use. Conclude the meeting with this prayer or one of your own choosing.

Hail to you, Mary,
who are wholly united to the redeeming consecration of your Son!

Mother of the Church,
enlighten the people of God along the paths of faith, hope, and love.
Help us live in the truth of the consecration of Christ
for the entire human family of the modern world.

In entrusting to you, O Mother,
the world, all individuals, and peoples,
we also entrust to you this very consecration of the world,
placing it in your motherly heart.

Immaculate Heart of Mary,
help us to conquer the menace of evil,
which so easily takes root in the hearts of people today,
and whose immeasurable effects
already weigh down upon our modern world
and seem to block the paths toward the future.

From famine and war, deliver us.
From nuclear war, from incalculable self-destruction, from every kind
    of war, deliver us.
From sins against human life from its very beginning, deliver us.
From hatred and from the demeaning of the dignity of the children of
    God, deliver us.
From every kind of injustice in the life of society, both national and
    international, deliver us.
From readiness to trample on the commandments of God, deliver us.
From attempts to stifle in human hearts the very truth of God, deliver
    us.
From the loss of awareness of good and evil, deliver us.
From sins against the Holy Spirit, deliver us.

Accept, O Mother of Christ,
this cry laden with the sufferings of all individual human beings,
and with the sufferings of whole societies.

Help us with the power of the Holy Spirit to conquer all sin:
    individual sin and the "sin of the world," sin in all its
    manifestations.
Let there be revealed once more in the history of the world
the infinite saving power of the redemption: the power of merciful
    love.
May it put a stop to evil.
May it transform consciences.
May your immaculate heart reveal for all the light of hope.
Amen.

SIX

The Family and Parish Ministry

Individual use. This chapter focuses on how families minister to one another.

Group use. You will need Bibles, newsprint, and markers for this session. Begin with a prayer. Then have each person answer these two questions: "What role has the parish played in your life? How has your relationship to the parish changed over the years?" Then silently read through this section.

Until the nineteenth century, Catholicism was a relatively minor denomination in the United States. In this pioneer Church, the family was the basic unit of Catholic education and devotional life. Early immigrants gathered for worship in the homes of wealthy Catholics. As the number of Catholics increased, parishes were formed, but the home remained the center of Catholic prayer, devotion, and religious instruction. Near the end of the last century, new parish organizations and devotions began, and many Catholic practices shifted from home to parish. Struggling immigrant families gathered in the neighborhood parish to learn, to worship, to socialize, to work for neighborhood change, and to educate their children. This organizational, devotional parish became the norm until Vatican Council II.

Since Vatican II, social changes have brought about changes in parish life and structure. Today, Catholics account for about 28 percent of the total United States population and are found in all echelons of society, business, and politics. New waves of Catholic immigrants—Vietnamese, Mong (from Cambodia), Cuban, Central American, and others—have arrived here. Although the number of Catholics is increasing, vocations to the priesthood and religious communities are in decline. At the same time, secularism and high mobility create a rootless feeling among many middle-class families.

In the midst of these changes, Church leaders are taking a fresh look at the parish. Although most active Catholics still belong to a parish, many no longer see the parish as the hub of family activities. People want today's parish to help them establish relationships, integrate varied aspects of their lives, handle individual and family pressures, recognize their gifts, and support family life. The changing landscape of Catholic life indicates that the family is again becoming a more significant focus of religious instruction, prayer, and devotion in the parish.

Parishes struggle to focus on this new centrality of the family. And yet, people of all ages, races, and economic conditions still need to feel welcome in the parish. The parish priest, in a special way, sets the tone for a parish's welcome. His liturgical style and his preaching are critically important. The Sunday liturgy is the only time most people have regular contact with the parish.

Jack, Margaret, and their teenagers, Fred and Sally, moved into a parish, registered, and received envelopes. But when they went to parish functions, they felt out of place. When they attended Mass, they felt like strangers.

One day, Fred and Sally shocked their parents when they asked for permission to attend the local Protestant church. That Protestant community made those young people *feel* welcomed and a part of the group.

How the Christian community treats people affects their attitudes toward the Church. Many Catholics join other denominations because of neglect and insensitive treatment at times of engagement, divorce, or a child's baptism. For instance, Hispanic leaders express concern that many Spanish-speaking people, coming from strong Catholic backgrounds, are lost to other denominations more hospitable and sensitive to the Hispanic needs.

Many Catholic parishes are responding to the challenge of becoming nurturing, caring communities of faith. This is especially important at life's special events such as birth, death, marriage, new parish membership, sickness, divorce, and loss of a job. Here is an example of how parish support helped Bev through her divorce.

"When it happened," Bev said, "my pastor and neighbors supported me and encouraged my participation in parish activities. Our family was well known in the parish, and the first time I came to Mass after my husband filed for divorce, I felt nervous and self-conscious but never unwelcome. Parish support helped me greatly through this painful time."

No one is an island. All humans need relationships to survive. When people feel wanted, they are more committed. The experiences of being welcomed and wanted link people together and help create meaning. It is easy to see why welcome and hospitality are starting points in parish outreach to families.

Individual use. Use this section to explore how your parish welcomes people.

1. Reflect upon a significant event or a crisis in your life when the parish supported you. Describe what happened.

Group use. Use newsprint to record the participants' answers to items 2, 3, and 4. You might want to bring some of the group's responses to the attention of appropriate parish leaders.

2. Make a list of the various groups of people in your parish (for example, young families, single adults, children, senior citizens, the widowed, the divorced, and the like). Next to each group, write what you think each group expects from the parish.

3. What are specific things your parish does to make people feel welcome?

4. How can your parish become a more hospitable and welcoming community? Give specific suggestions.

Family Priorities

Group use. Take turns reading this section aloud.

Parish family ministry begins with the recognition that each family possesses its own identity and special gifts. Then, parish leaders need to discern family strengths and weaknesses. Today it is more difficult to address family concerns than it was a generation ago. Until recently, the average Catholic family experienced close family and ethnic ties.

Husbands worked, wives stayed at home, and children usually received a Catholic parochial-school education. Most Catholics went to Sunday Mass, ate no meat on Friday, and often said the rosary together. They acknowledged and tried to obey the Church's laws on premarital sex, birth control, and divorce. Today this picture has changed. And so, the parish must shift its orientation to meet family needs more effectively.

Almost every family has a hectic schedule. There is a growing number of single-parent families and families where both parents work. Job responsibilities, school activities, home maintenance, nurturing family relationships, sports and other recreational activities, along with parish commitments all compete for the family's time and energies.

The contemporary parish also follows a hectic schedule. In addition to its regular schedule of Masses and confessions, many parishes have numerous meetings, committees, building projects, and educational functions. Most parish activities serve the family in one way or another. Unless the parish takes into account the real rhythm of family life, it can actually detract from the family.

Jill told me her pastor had urged her to teach religion to junior high school students. She had already turned down the same request from the parish religious education director. "I already spend three evenings a week at the parish counting money, attending choir practice, and serving on various committees. What should I tell the pastor?" she wondered.

Jill not only refused to teach the class but also phased out several other parish activities that kept her away from the family. The teaching request helped her sort out what was happening to family relationships because of her parish involvement. Parish pressures were making it difficult for Jill to be with her family.

This might not have happened to Jill if her parish centered its vision around families and their needs. Concern about family relationships should lead a parish to develop policies that welcome and involve families but do not burden family members with parish activities. Parish leaders must work together to create programs in line with family priorities.

Families need intimacy to grow, and family intimacy depends on the *quality* time members spend together. The emphasis here is on quality. Some people who spend a great deal of time in another's presence never develop intimacy. Quality relationships demand space and time away from the pressures of everyday life. Parishes can help families work toward family intimacy by encouraging a home-rooted family spirituality.

People also need a variety of liturgical and prayer experiences. Sunday liturgy alone does not satisfy spiritual hunger for an entire week.

Not that long ago, private devotions such as the rosary, novenas, and benediction were vital to Catholic identity and life-style. These devotions stressed popular piety—devotions arising from the heritage of ordinary people. More recently, the development of a popular liturgy in the language of the people caused a decline in the promotion of some devotions—morning or evening prayers, the rosary, stations of the cross, mealtime prayers, and other devotions that formerly filled the lives of Catholics. But many Catholics still speak of their faith in terms of morning and mealtime prayers, ashes, Advent wreaths, and family devotions. Families often create personalized ways to teach their children about God. Parish leaders should encourage new forms of family spirituality that anchor parish life.

One such practice could be devotion to the Holy Family. Families can relate to Mary as a model for today's people—a woman of faith, struggling through ambiguity with perseverance and trust. They can look to Joseph as a man of integrity, faithfulness, and sensitivity. Parish leaders can also encourage families to lean on one another for support. In this way, spirituality in one home can spread from family to family. This shared spirituality will affect the liturgical and sacramental experience in the parish.

Individual use. "Family Priorities," "Family Devotions," and "Displaying Your Catholic Heritage" are good activities to complement these questions.

Group use. Use these questions as discussion starters.

1.   What activities compete for your family's time and interest?

2.   Review the activities listed under question 1 and assign a priority rating to each one *(1* being the most important). How do you feel about this list? Are there any changes you want to make?

3.   What religious devotions does your family practice?

4.   How does your family home and current life-style reflect your Catholic heritage?

Parish Support

Group use. Take some private time to read this section and then write your answers to question 1.

Every family has survival and intimacy needs. These needs center around affirming family values, supporting family growth, and providing a network of human connections. But the family depends on the broader community, including the local parish, to help meet these needs.

People first discover God in family relationships—couples with each other, parents with children, children with parents, sisters and brothers with one another. These bonds influence each person's response to the perennial question, "How am I *with* God?" A person's response to this question changes over time. It is always shaped by the quality of relationships among family members, friends, work associates, and neighbors. Pastoral ministers help by offering meaningful liturgies and other prayer experiences, catechetical programs, and a variety of parish activities.

One area in which adults look to the parish for assistance is in educating their children. In the recent past, many parents gave this responsibility to teachers in the parish schools and CCD programs. Today, with the help of pastoral leaders, parents see themselves as the primary catechists of their children. Parents realize that their words and actions keep the great story of God's love alive in their families. They count on the parochial school or parish religious education program to provide a more structured and systematic approach to Catholic beliefs and practices.

Today, people want a unified religion program—one that makes no distinction between children in the parochial school and children in the CCD program. All children are welcome in the parish and deserve a good education. To create this environment, parish priests, the school principal, teachers, and the director of religious education must all work together.

Parishes can devise creative ways to help parents connect what the children learn in the parish's religious education programs with their home and neighborhood experiences. Catechesis happens naturally whenever family members share their understanding of Catholic belief and practices. A love for Scripture is central to this learning. Parish leaders can encourage families to purchase a Bible, place it in a prominent spot in the home, and use it on a regular basis. Bulletin inserts can help parents make connections between their beliefs and current events. Parents can learn to use television programs, media events, newspaper accounts, magazine articles, and advertisements to discuss Catholic beliefs and values.

In addition to the customary catechetical programs, many parishes offer family programs. There are many different models for family learning. A successful one is the family cluster in which a number of families join together on a regular basis to share faith, break bread, and enjoy one another's company. Families usually take turns organizing the meetings.

As parents become more aware of their responsibilities, they look to the Church for help. Many parishes respond to parents' needs by offering a variety of adult education programs that support family values. These programs include classes in Scripture, conscience formation, family dynamics, communication skills, time management for families, and stress reduction.

Families rely on the Church for more than instruction. During times of stress and brokenness, the family often seeks help from the parish. Leaders should be familiar with local, state, and governmental agencies that provide services such as career counseling, senior citizens' programs, food and housing assistance, medical help, and unemployment assistance. Some parishes open their facilities to self-help groups such as Alcoholics Anonymous, Alanon, and Adult Children of Alcoholics. Others publish the location of these groups in their parish bulletins.

Many families approach parish leaders with problems requiring counseling skills. When a family needs counseling, it often does not know where to turn for help. Most people hesitate to phone an unknown counselor or walk into an agency. If they belong to a parish, they may seek help from a priest, deacon, director of religious education, or youth minister. A competent minister knows when to recommend professional help and where to direct people. Timing is important. To suggest therapy too soon frightens many people away. Karen's story illustrates the need to listen before giving advice.

Soon after her divorce, Karen moved into a new parish. She had little money and a son to support. Not knowing where to turn, Karen approached her new pastor.

Father Ted offered Karen a secretarial job in the parish. After a few weeks, Karen felt competent in her new position, but she wasn't making any friends. To make matters worse, her son's teacher began to complain about his behavior. Discouraged, Karen once again turned to her pastor. After listening for a few minutes, he abruptly said, "There is nothing I can do to help you. You need professional counseling." With that, he quickly gave her the name and phone number of a counselor and ushered her out of his office.

Karen left the pastor's office feeling misunderstood, ashamed, and embarrassed. She was not ready to hear the pastor's advice, and she felt he had not heard her concerns.

A good parish minister needs many skills to avoid the kind of situation Karen found herself in. Most pastoral formation programs include courses in *listening* skills. Other parish leaders, motivated by their own experiences, seek to develop these skills elsewhere. Parish staffs often invite members of local counseling agencies to speak at their staff meetings. Parish leaders then compile a list of qualified counselors with varied backgrounds and skills. Many counselors or counseling agencies will work closely with a support group, such as the parish. Some provide free consultation to pastors and other leaders who are concerned about specific parishioners. With such help, parish leaders can determine the best way to approach a person or family in need of counseling.

Another concern is the cost of therapy. Most businesses provide family health insurance coverage that includes mental health services. Some people do not know this, but parish leaders can bring it to their attention. Unfortunately, since mental health coverage is often not full coverage, families worry about making up the difference. Parish leaders should know the names of counselors willing to accept clients with low incomes or little medical coverage. Some parishes set aside money to help

families afford counseling services. Many dioceses sponsor counseling programs through Catholic Charities or other family life offices. Parish bulletins can provide this information.

Parish family ministry recognizes that every person belongs to a family. Even single people living alone and freely bonded families fit in somewhere. The parish's definition of family should embrace everyone, not just primary families. Single people and married couples, for instance, have much to offer one another. Young adult groups have witnessed the benefits of mixing these two groups together.

When Ellen began a young adult ministry in her parish, she debated whether to include married couples or to restrict the group to young singles. She finally decided to open the doors to singles, divorced people, and couples.

Fifty people attended the first meeting. Excitement filled the air as young people planned future activities. Single people outnumbered married couples, but there was a good representation of both groups.

A few weeks after the first meeting, a college student approached Ellen and thanked her for starting the group. She told Ellen, "My mother and father lived in a very stormy marriage until they divorced. Their divorce made it difficult for me to date men. I was afraid the same thing would happen to me. But meeting Mark and Jan in this group has been great. Their marriage is good because they work at it. They are teaching me that couples can be happy together."

Ellen's story shows the importance of mixing single and married people together. A good family mix, including singles, married people, intact families, single-parent families, remarried families, widows and widowers provides an opportunity for people to learn from one another. In the process, people are drawn into a common experience of extended family.

One way in which parishes can support intergenerational relationships is by inviting grandparents and other relatives to attend social and prayer experiences together. My own mother is very close to all of her grandchildren, including those in college. She is the heart of our extended family. It is wonderful when parishes provide spiritual opportunities for Mom, her grandchildren, and people like her.

All parish ministry must begin by discerning people's needs. This is especially true of family ministry. If real needs are not met, family members might say, "What happens in this parish may be nice for some people, but not for us." Singles, divorced people, and bereaved families, for instance, have real needs that must be identified before parishes can make an impact on their lives. The Christian community must first get a clear picture of its families and their needs. Once those needs are known, the community can make a real difference.

Group use. When you have answered question 1, use questions 2 and 3 for discussion purposes. Then take a break.

1. How would you answer the question, "How am I *with* God?"

2. How are parents involved in the parish school or religious education program?

Individual use. You might find some useful suggestions in the "Activities" section of this chapter.

3. What kinds of family programs or ministries would you like to see developed in your parish? How can you help bring them about?

Family Helping Family

Group use. Take turns reading this section aloud. Then discuss the questions at the end of the section.

The family-helping-family approach to ministry gives new hope to Christian families. When services are not available through public agencies, the parish can create a network of service from local parish talent.

Once our pastor asked my father to provide clothes for a poor family from the stock in his dry-goods store. Dad had been giving clothes and food to the poor for years, but this was the first time the parish had asked him to do it. He was delighted. He would be helping someone from his own parish. Dad never knew which family he had helped, but he was glad someone had asked him to contribute.

Most parishes have social workers, plumbers, doctors, nurses, shopkeepers, carpenters, business executives, and teachers who, if they were asked, would gladly offer (within limits) their time and talent to help the broader parish community. People like this are a resource pool for family ministry. Investments of time, energy, and talent, as well as money all help make people feel part of the parish.

There are many different ways to involve people in helping families. One popular way is the Advent Giving Tree.

One year, the family life committee of a small parish decided to have a Giving Tree during Advent. Two major companies had just closed, leaving many people in the parish and neighborhood community unemployed. The committee members contacted parish leaders and asked them to suggest names of people who might need assistance. After receiving the names, the committee chose Joanne to make the necessary contacts. Joanne was well known and respected in the community.

Joanne went about her task with great enthusiasm and care. Because she respected people's need for confidentiality, Joanne assured each person that the gifts would be given anonymously. She then asked each family about their needs. Often, families requested items only for their children. Joanne, however, always included something for the parents as well.

Children in the parish school and religious education program made ornaments. Joanne compiled a master list with a number for each separate item, followed by the name of the family member who would receive the gift. She put only the identifying number and a description of the gift on the ornament.

More than two hundred ornaments hung on the tree the first Sunday of Advent. At each Mass, the lector announced the meaning of the Giving Tree and asked people to choose an ornament. They were instructed to wrap the gift, attach the identifying ornament to the package, and return it by a specific date. Parishioners took all of the ornaments by the end of the early morning Masses, leaving none for the later Masses. It was enlightening to watch how families made their choices. Often little children helped their parents make a decision. One family of all boys chose an ornament gift for a little girl, because they hoped some day to have a sister.

The gifts were beautifully wrapped. Some people gave the suggested item and attached an additional, unrequested gift. Some ornaments asked for food certificates of specified amounts. Many parishioners gave more. From the many people who volunteered to deliver the gifts, the committee chose those who would be most sensitive to each family's need for privacy.

This successful venture became a cherished parish tradition. In its second year, people began calling the parish office in September, offering to help with the Giving Tree. One woman told the parish secretary, "Last year, our family was in dire straights, because my husband was out of work. The gifts we received from the parish meant so much. This year, we are in a better financial situation and want to do something for a needy family. How can we help with the Giving Tree?"

This parish knows what it means to be a Church family and, at the same time, knows how to support its families. There are many other ways to create this kind of parish environment. One effective way is through peer ministry.

Both secular and religious worlds know the benefits of peer counseling and peer ministry. Both involve people having similar concerns. For example, people who have experienced a death in the family are often the best people to console someone who has just lost a child or a spouse. This holds true for people in alcoholic families, parents having difficulties with their teenagers, divorced people, single parents, and others. The same principle also applies to teenagers ministering to other teenagers.

One parish, located near a large military base, asked some retired military personnel to set up a program to welcome and support new military families during their temporary stay in the parish. These retirees remembered their own difficulties in making roots in new places. Although the parish had a welcoming committee, the people setting up the program recognized that military families have special needs and concerns that can best be addressed by other military families.

Parishes that encourage its members to help one another usually thrive. They assist families in recognizing their gifts, talents, and skills.

They then challenge family members to use these gifts for God's larger family.

Individual use. If you are not already involved in your parish, see how you can use your talents and skills to help other people.

1. In what ways does your parish affirm and use the talents and skills of its parishioners to help other parishioners?

2. What kinds of professional and skilled labor are represented in your parish?

3. How can your parish better use its human resources to support family ministry?

Family Stories

Group use. Have a good storyteller from the group read this section aloud, while everyone else follows along.

In the final analysis, family identity and purpose are best discovered in family stories. In all aspects of parish life—from homilies to catechesis, from spiritual-enrichment programs to parish picnics—Church ministers need to encourage people to discover God in their own stories. The following event illustrates the significance of family stories.

For one whole year, our family looked forward to a trip to Daytona Beach. Each week, Dad set aside twenty dollars for the trip. The day before our vacation was to begin, a wall in the family store collapsed. Dad was worried about repairing it but finally decided to proceed with the trip. He didn't want to disappoint us.

After we drove through the Great Smoky Mountains, Dad got sick. By the time we arrived at Daytona Beach, he had lost control of the right side of his body.

Dad went to a doctor who told him there was pressure on his inner ear. We rented a motel room on the beach but were very concerned about Dad. He was walking with great difficulty and was clearly in pain. Still, he wanted us to have a good time. I heard Dad tell Mom, "The kids looked forward to Florida all year. Let's stay a few days. I'll be all right."

One evening, we went to a restaurant for dinner. As Mom and I helped Dad into his chair, a woman stared at us and said to her family, "Look! Isn't that disgusting. That man is so drunk they have to hold him up." We said nothing, but her words pierced our hearts.

Two days later, we started home. My sister and I drove. During the long trek back to Ohio, Daytona Beach was rarely mentioned. We were too concerned about Dad. His health was more important than our vacation. After returning to Cincinnati, he received medical treatment and eventually recovered.

As a teenager, I did not grasp the meaning and extent of my parents' sacrifice for our family. As an adult, I see more clearly their love and God's presence in our family story. I now know the importance of remembering and cherishing these stories.

Children like stories and pictures of family members. Older adults enjoy remembering both the happy and the sad times. One successful method of storytelling directs the participants to write down significant life events. Based on these events, each person develops a faith line, helping the individual see God in his or her life story. This method shows how people can discover God through their own personal and familial stories. When God is found, the unsung efforts of family members take on new meaning.

Before my father died, I wanted to gather memorable pictures from our family photo albums and put them into a book. On Thanksgiving Day, we sat in the living room, and Dad started to tell stories. At first, I paid little attention, concentrating instead on a televised football game. Soon, I realized what was happening, turned away from the TV set, and listened.

I never made the memorial book, but to this day, I cherish my decision to listen to Dad as he summarized the history of our family. I don't remember individual stories, but I remember the significance of the moment. That's the way it is with family stories. They have a way of bringing family members together.

Time and again as I write, preach, and lecture, I hear Mom saying, "Bob, tell stories!" My parents stressed the power of storytelling in family life, for this is how every family learns Jesus' story. God is present in family stories. They recall the Word-made-flesh in everyday life. Families grow together through joys and struggles which find a focal point in the Gospel story. When families realize this, family stories and the Holy Family story become one. When parishes appreciate God's presence in family stories, the universal Church and the domestic Church become one.

Group use. Discuss these questions as a group. Some people may need to use a Bible. End the meeting by discussing how this program has helped you.

1. What is your favorite Scripture story?

2. Does this story relate in some way to your family story? Explain.

Individual use. To help bring your family together, consider sharing family stories one evening during mealtime.

3. What is one story you remember from your childhood? Describe it here.

4. Why is this story important to you now?

5. What does this story tell you about your family?

Activities

Individual or group use. Choose one or more activities to do with your family. Some of the activities can be done in family clusters.

Because this chapter focuses on parish family ministry, some activities include suggestions for parish implementation. Others center on home projects. Family priorities will determine which kind of activity is better for your family. Of course, your family might want to design its own activity.

Family Hospitality. If someone has recently moved into your neighborhood or parish, consider ways to welcome him or her. Some suggestions include (1) dropping by to visit and bringing some cookies, (2) phoning the person to find out if he or she needs assistance, (3) inviting the new person (or family) to your home for dinner, and (4) offering to accompany the newcomer to Mass or some special parish function.

Family Night.   Parents often get caught up in the activities of work, raising children, and maintaining a household. This activity invites families with children to slow the pace of life and to spend some special time together. Choose any night of the week that is good for your family (or perhaps a Saturday or Sunday afternoon) and designate it as Family Night. Make it a family tradition and try to stick to the same night and time each week. Determine a simple format for the evening, such as an opening prayer, a family activity, a snack, entertainment, and time for sharing.

Family Clusters.   The family cluster is a way of gathering people, children as well as adults, for a time of sharing faith and one another's company. The idea is to form a small network of families that commit themselves to journey in faith over a specific period of time. The families choose a regular meeting time (for example, the first Friday of the month). The place can be rotated or remain stable. The format can be the one suggested for Family Night, or you can use some of the many other activities suggested in this book. You might consider asking one of the parish priests to celebrate Mass for your cluster, or designate one evening as family story time. Families can take turns leading the meeting.

Displaying Your Catholic Heritage.   People's surroundings often reflect their values. Examine your home to see how it shows your Catholic heritage. Every family has its own style. Some suggestions for improving the Catholic look of your home include hanging religious art or posters, subscribing to Catholic magazines or newspapers, and displaying the family Bible.

Family Devotions.   Growing up Catholic can be the source of enjoyable customs and devotions. If you are not using any of them now, consider reintroducing some devotions to your family. Say the rosary together, pray with children at bedtime, bless one another before going to bed, pause before mealtime prayers, or the like.

Faith Line.   This activity is especially good for adults, senior citizens, and single people. Draw a faith line representing how your faith has developed over the years. Have the line go up for times of positive growth and down for low points in your spiritual development. Go back and indicate what each high and low symbolizes. If you do this alone, consider sharing some of your thoughts and feelings with a trusted friend or relative.

Family Priorities. This activity helps establish family priorities. It requires a large sheet of paper, a marker, some index cards, and pencils. Gather the family together and ask everyone to brainstorm family activities and responsibilities—including work, school, and so forth. List each item on a large sheet of paper. For each item listed, give everyone one index card. (For example, if your family listed twenty items, each person receives twenty index cards.) Have everyone write each item on a separate index card and then put the cards in order of priority and number them. This part of the activity should be done without consulting other family members. When everyone is finished, ask each person, in turn, to read his or her list. Record each item's number on the large sheet of paper. When all lists have been shared, add the numbers and determine the family's top five priorities (that is, the five items with the lowest numbers). The results may cause some disagreement among family members, so allow time for sharing and discussing.

Parish Hospitality. Join a committee to welcome new parishioners. If one does not exist in your parish, start one. Some possibilities for welcoming newcomers include: (1) an introduction at Mass once a month, followed by coffee and donuts after Mass; (2) a Newcomers Evening, sponsored on a regular basis (for instance, once a month, quarterly, or once a year); or (3) a wine and cheese party (include soft drinks) to welcome all newcomers. Send out invitations and assign a veteran parishioner to sponsor a newcomer. The veteran parishioners should follow up the written invitations with a phone call and accompany the newcomers to the event. Introduce the pastor during the event. Allow parish council members or other parish leaders to provide information on parish activities. Encourage the newcomers to meet other parish members.

Assessing Needs. One way to assess parish family needs informally is to ask people at all the Masses one weekend to fill out a card stating what they think the parish needs in the way of family ministry. This activity should be announced in the parish bulletin and included in church announcements. Members of the family life committee, the parish council, or some other organization can tally the responses and determine which suggestions are repeated most often. Announce the results in the bulletin and form a planning committee to implement the suggestions.

Prayer

The "Hear, O Israel" prayer is the cornerstone of Jewish prayer. It was the daily prayer of Jesus, his family, and the disciples. Psalm 95 is often used as a morning prayer.

Individual use. Here is a prayer you can use to start the day. Since the prayer is an ancient one, you will be participating in a custom that the Holy Family probably cherished.

Hear, O Israel, the Lord is our God, the Lord is One!
Blessed is God's glorious kingdom for ever and ever!

Come, let us sing joyfully to the Lord;
    let us acclaim the Rock of our salvation.
Let us greet him with thanksgiving;
    let us joyfully sing psalms to him.
For the Lord is a great God,
    and a great king above all gods;
In his hands are the depths of the earth,
    and the tops of mountains are his.
His is the sea, for he has made it,
    and the dry land, which his hands have formed.
Amen.

Epilog

The journey toward God is an invitation to freedom. But freedom never comes easily. Sometimes joyful, sometimes painful, life's path cannot be traveled alone.

Since stories are essential to family life, *Holy Family* concludes with two anecdotes. The first speaks of freeing family members through love, and the second, of remembering simple family moments.

Beth, a teenager, hurt inside because of a problem she faced. She arrived early for Mass one Sunday and sat alone. Shortly before the liturgy began, a young mother with a baby sat beside her.

During Mass, Beth thought of her problem and began to cry. As tears rolled down her cheeks, the baby leaned over and wiped them away, one at a time. When Beth looked at the baby, the infant was smiling.

After Mass, Beth left church and the mother followed her. "Would you stop for a moment?" the mother said. "I want to thank you for what you did for my baby."

Surprised, Beth replied, "I don't understand. I should thank you. Your baby really helped me. When she wiped away my tears, I forgot about my problem. How did I help your baby?"

The mother answered, "Megan had a very difficult birth, and in spite of all the love our family has shown her, she has never smiled—until this morning when she wiped away your tears."

Beth then looked into the eyes of the smiling baby, whose face said that life is good. The grateful mother told Beth, "Today, my baby smiled for the first time. Now Megan is really alive. She is free." Beth knew that she was also set free that morning.

Freedom is often most evident in people helping one another. Whenever people share who they are and what they possess, they are choosing to love. Love, the source of freedom, reveals itself in simple moments.

Joan grew up on a midwestern farm, where strong family ties and hard work characterized her early life. She left the farm years ago, but she occasionally returns to visit her parents.

During one such visit, Joan's dad noticed that her shoes needed fixing. Together, they went into his shoe shop to mend them. Smiling, her dad said, "I'll make a cobbler out of you yet." These simple words struck a cord in Joan's heart. The tap, tap of the hammer symbolized the years of joy and sorrow their family shared. In a flash, Joan saw how her parents fashioned the feet upon which she walks in freedom and molded the heart that helps her love. With that legacy, Joan can provide feet and hearts for others.

People need to set aside time to appreciate the gift of family. These moments will help a person understand how the journey toward God is on a family road. The simple human actions of wiping tears and mending shoes are signposts that can keep everybody headed in the right direction.

Acknowledgments

Olivia Hater, my mother, for reading the manuscript, offering valuable suggestions, and encouraging me to finish this book.

Richard Haubner, Sister Jeanette Jabour, O.P., Sister Marie Antoine Humpert, and my many colleagues and friends for helping me formulate my ideas while writing this book.

Joanne Beirise and Joanne Miller for typing the original manuscript.

Margaret Dodds, the editor from Tabor Publishing, for suggesting the final format of this book, arranging it, contributing significantly to the text, and adding discussion questions, activities, and margin notes.

Photo Credits